Go!

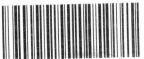

Go!

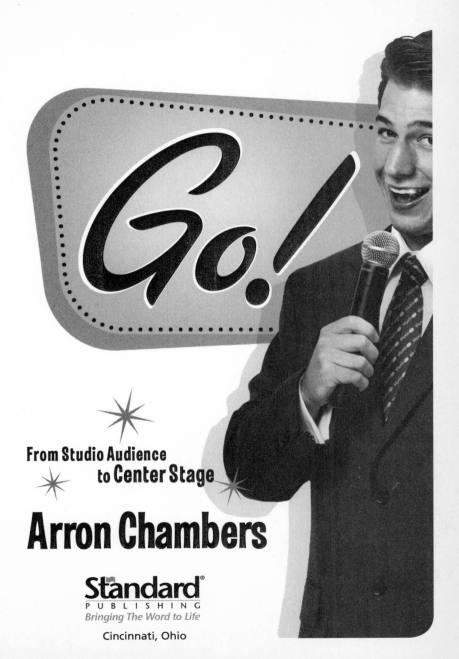

From Studio Audience to Center Stage

Arron Chambers

Standard®
PUBLISHING
Bringing The Word to Life

Cincinnati, Ohio

Published by Standard Publishing, Cincinnati, Ohio

www.standardpub.com

Project editor: Lynn Lusby Pratt

Cover and interior design: Brand Navigation

ISBN 978-0-7847-2282-4

Library of Congress Cataloging-in-Publication Data

Chambers, Arron.

Go! : from studio audience to center stage / Arron Chambers.

p. cm.

Includes bibliographical references.

ISBN 978-0-7847-2282-4 (perfect bound)

1. Christian life. 2. Television game shows. I. Title.

BV4501.3.C427 2009

248.4--dc22

2008037751

15 14 13 12 11 10 09 9 8 7 6 5 4 3 2 1

To Mark Tyre and Keith Simmons—
my friends and fellow slaw-dog connoisseurs.

Your wisdom made me a better leader.

Your example made me a better minister.

Your faith made me a better Christ follower.

Your friendship made me a better man.

I'll always cherish the time we spent serving together on center stage.

Table of Contents

Come on Down!

introduction

Are you happy where you are?

My friend Sara was . . . and she wasn't.

Sure, Sara was happy to be in sunny, southern California while on winter break during her senior year of college, sitting with her friends in the studio audience of the hit TV game show *The Price Is Right.* It was incredibly exciting simply to be in the audience, but she wanted more.

She and her friends had traveled to California from the mountains of east Tennessee for the sole purpose of getting on *The Price Is Right.* So on the first day of their visit, they awoke at 4:00 AM, donned the matching shirts they had made to help them stand out, and went to the studio to get in line by 5:00 AM—but it was already too late. The line was full and they couldn't get in. Undeterred, they decided they needed to get in line earlier and lined up again at eight o'clock that night. There were already sixteen people ahead of them.

Sara and her friends camped out on the sidewalk all that night. When the doors to the studio opened at six-thirty the next morning, there were four hundred people in line with them. Only the first three hundred people were allowed to enter and take their places in a second line!

While in the second line, Sara and her friends were given tickets and moved to a third line where they were divided into groups of seven and interviewed by a producer of the show.

The producer asked people about themselves—trying to decide which ones might be entertaining contestants. Sara, desperate to get on center stage, told the producer that when she grew up she wanted his job. He smiled and seemed genuinely impressed. Sara felt hopeful that her dream would come true.

She wasn't content just to sit in the audience; Sara wanted to be on center stage. She wanted to stand next to Bob Barker. She wanted to compete for cash and prizes. She wanted to spin the Big Wheel. She wanted to be in the Showcase Showdown at the end of the show—and win both showcases! Then Sara wanted to sit in her shiny new car . . . and in the sleek boat she'd just won—surrounded by Barker's Beauties and waving like a fourth-grade school girl as the camera moved in for a close-up. Finally, the credits would run across the TV screen, and Bob Barker would remind the audience: "To help control the pet population, have your pets spayed or neutered."

But the only way all that was going to happen would be for Rich Fields to call her name: "Sara Manny, come on down!"

Created for Center Stage

God has already called your name. Whether you know it or not, he's chosen you to leave the audience and go to center stage.

The apostle Paul said this about us: "We are God's workmanship, created in Christ Jesus to do good works, which God prepared in advance for us to do" (Ephesians 2:10).

It has always been God's plan for us to leave the audience. He didn't design us to sit anonymously in the shadows forever, just beyond the reach of the spotlight. No, we were created to stand on the center stage of life and do something extraordinarily good for God. So even before he created the first eardrum, he cried out for all who would have ears to hear, "Come on down!"

Can you hear your Savior calling?

Well . . . what are you going to do?

Life is full of choices.

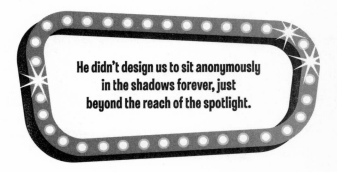

He didn't design us to sit anonymously in the shadows forever, just beyond the reach of the spotlight.

Gayle Grinds made a choice.

In 1998, she chose to get comfortable on her couch . . . and not move . . . for six years![1]

Gayle lived in Stuart, Florida, with a man named Herman who tried to get her off that couch many times but just couldn't. So he gave up—and at some point, so did she. At first, she could have gotten up but chose not to. She was comfortable. She had plenty to eat. There was always something to watch on TV. She was happy where she was. She had most everything she needed within arm's distance, so she lived on that couch. If you can call what she was doing *living*.

When rescue workers were called to her house six years later, they were horrified by the scene. The stench was so overwhelming that everyone who went into the house had to wear protective gear, but that wasn't the worst part. Gayle had sat on that couch for so long that her skin had grafted with the fabric. She and the couch had become one.

Sadly, Gayle Laverne Grinds died in August 2004, still attached to that couch.

What a grotesque tragedy.

I think it's just as tragic for Christians to get comfortable in a church seat . . . and not move . . . for decades.

Sadly, many lost people will die because too many Christians are too attached to their church seats.

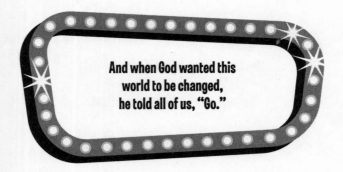

And when God wanted this world to be changed, he told all of us, "Go."

Have you and your favorite seat at church become one?

Do you think the challenge to reach the lost is someone else's to accept?

Do you think you've done enough already and it's another person's turn?

Do you think that the starving people in Darfur are the problem of the locals?

Do you think that the AIDS crisis is best handled by professionals?

Do you think that you're really too busy to serve food to the homeless at the rescue mission downtown?

If so, I've got news for you. God never intended for us to sit comfortably on our seats while this fallen world falls apart all around us.

Trust God and Go

Throughout all time, whenever God saw a need, when he had a plan, when there was something he wanted done . . . he told someone to go.

When God wanted to establish a nation, he told Abram, "Go."

When God wanted to defeat the Midianites, he told Gideon, "Go."

When God wanted to bless Hannah, he told her, "Go."

When God wanted to deliver his people through Esther, he told her, "Go."

When God wanted the disciples to know of Christ's resurrection, he had the angel tell the women, "Go."

When God wanted the disciples to get to work sharing the gospel, he told them, "Go."

When God wanted the apostles to keep preaching in the temple courts, he told them, "Go."

When God wanted Paul to hear about Jesus Christ, he told Ananias, "Go."

And when God wanted this world to be changed, he told all of us, "Go."

We're going to study each of these callings, and we're going to learn that God doesn't want us to sit in the audience; he wants us on center stage.

I believe we have a divine appointment. We are audience to both unbelievable need and unbelievable opportunity. With the amount of information we receive (and have access to) 24/7, we can no longer say, "We didn't know." And with what any Bible-believing Christian knows about God, we can never say, "God can't" or "We can't."

God can.

God will.

So we must.

We must get off the couch, answer the call, and go.

If we'll open our eyes, we'll see that God is doing amazing things in every corner of this world and he wants us to join him. See what God can do when ordinary people—like you and me—choose to leave the comfort of the audience of life. Got designed us for center stage.

That's where Sara wanted to be. She wasn't content sitting comfortably in the audience; she wanted more. So when the music began and Bob Barker walked onto center stage, Sara joined the crowd in cheering with all her might. The roar of the crowd was louder than anything she had ever heard before. It was so loud, in fact, that she didn't hear when the announcer, Rich Fields, called out, "Sara Manny, come on down! You're the next contestant on *The Price Is Right!*" It wasn't until she saw a man on stage holding a card with her name on it that she realized she had been called.

All the work—the cost of the plane ticket, making the shirts, the night spent on the sidewalk, the three lines . . . it was all worth it, because she was being called out of the studio audience.

She knew that something amazing was happening. And she didn't have to think about it for one millisecond. The choice was obvious.

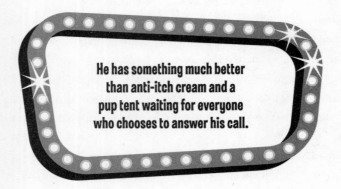

He has something much better than anti-itch cream and a pup tent waiting for everyone who chooses to answer his call.

Sara immediately answered the call, jumped to her feet, climbed over her girlfriends, left her place in the studio audience, and ran to the front of the studio—eventually making it all the way to center stage. She played Squeeze the Numbers and lost the grandfather clock, but won...(drumroll please!)... backpacking equipment and a year's supply of Gold Bond Medicated Ointment.

I have to pause here and make sure you know that God gives better gifts than Bob Barker.

Trust me.

Better yet, trust God.

He has something much better than anti-itch cream and a pup tent waiting for everyone who chooses to answer his call to leave the comfort of the audience for the excitement of center stage.

This is what he wanted all of his followers to know, so he told his disciples—who had left everything to serve with him on center stage: "Everyone who has left houses or brothers or sisters or father or mother or children or fields for my sake will receive a hundred times as much and will inherit eternal life" (Matthew 19:29).

What could be better than that? A hundred times more than what we left for Christ . . . *and* eternal life!

Why would anyone choose to sit in the audience with prizes like that available on center stage?

Your name is being called. Can you hear it? "______ (insert your name here), come on down!"

What are you going to do?

Don't think about it for even a millisecond. I pray you'll get up, get going, and get into the game.

Life is full of choices and this is yours: stay in the audience or join Jesus on center stage.

Are you happy where you are?

If not, come on down!

Let's go. Center stage awaits.

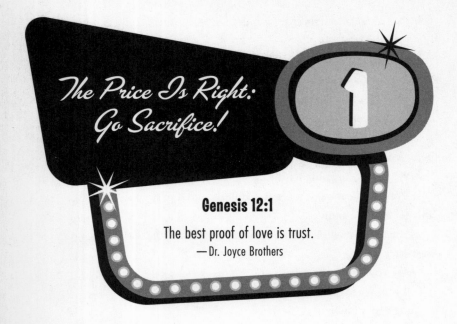

1

The Price Is Right: Go Sacrifice!

Genesis 12:1

The best proof of love is trust.
—Dr. Joyce Brothers

It's been called the world's largest yard sale. It's an Internet marketplace on which you can buy and sell almost anything you want. It's eBay.

Someone paid $263 for a piece of gum that Britney Spears spat out at a London Hotel.[1]

Another person paid $5.50 for an air guitar the owner said was "used once at a Bon Jovi concert in '89 for about three hours."[2]

One shopper paid $20,000 for a red, retired, Disney monorail.[3]

In June 2007, an ounce of lawn clippings sold for $46.[4]

The price of $30,000 was paid for advertising space on a young man's forehead.[5]

The online casino GoldenPalace.com paid $28,000 for a grilled cheese sandwich that supposedly bore the face of the virgin Mary.[6]

The "meaning of life" was for sale a few years ago. The "owner" wrote, "I have discovered the reason for our existence and will be happy to share this information with the highest bidder."[7] Someone paid $3.26 for this valuable information.

A pickle jar shaped like a cathedral was bought at a garage sale for $3.00—and turned out to be so rare that collectors knew of only five in the world. It then sold on eBay for $44,100.[8]

Who would pay $44,100 for a pickle jar?

Answer: Someone who thinks that a cathedral-shaped pickle jar is worth it.

Who would pay $263 for a piece of Britney Spears' chewing gum?

Answer: Someone who has no life!

What are you willing to pay for?

Are you willing to pay the price for your comfort? Are you willing to pay the price for your entertainment? Are you willing to pay the price for your financial advancement? Are you willing to pay the price for yourself?

One look at our bank statements, and we see a clear statement about what we value. Much of what I'm paying so much for doesn't matter all that much.

My flat-screen TV—which I sacrificed to pay for—makes watching Indianapolis Colts football games much more exciting, but it won't change my life.

My tailored Italian suit—which cost way too much—may help me look like I belong when in the company of "important" people or when conducting a wedding, but it does nothing to make my life truly meaningful.

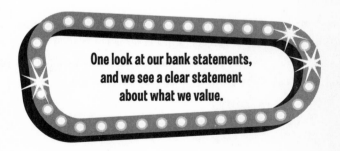

One look at our bank statements, and we see a clear statement about what we value.

My digital video recorder can record all my favorite shows with the press of a single button. I can also pause live TV so I can talk to my brother when he calls during *Lost* instead of letting his call go to voice mail after seeing his name on caller ID. I love it dearly because now I don't have to choose between the

Game Show Trivia

The Price Is Right is the longest running game show in television history.

two, but it won't improve the lives of starving orphans in Africa. I'm sacrificing monthly to pay for it like it really matters, but—in all seriousness—it doesn't matter at all.

We can become so blinded by this world that we lose sight of what really matters.

What really matters?

Family matters.

Friends matter.

Character matters.

People matter.

God matters.

Abraham believed this. So when God asked him to sacrifice everything, he thought the price was right.

The Call

It appears that Abraham was just minding his own business when God called him. From what we can see, Abraham (called Abram at the time) had done nothing of any consequence to be worthy—at least from our perspective—of being called by God to be the father of a "great nation" (Genesis 12:2).

He hadn't graduated from an accredited Bible college.

He had no impressive résumé.

He hadn't been the pastor of a megachurch.

He'd earned no honorary degrees, nor had he spoken at commencement services for an Ivy League school.

He'd never written a bestselling book. He'd never even *read* a bestselling book!

Game Show Trivia

The original emcee of *The Price Is Right*, Bill Cullen, appeared on the cover of *TV Guide* seven times, the record for a game show emcee.

He wasn't blogging daily, producing edgy videos, or speaking at the most popular conferences.

And he'd never been a father.

How could he be the father of a great nation when he'd never even been the father of a small family? Does that make any sense? Well, it does when we realize that God doesn't play by our rules.

Our rules say that we must accomplish a lot of important things before we get called to do something important. Based on what we see in the Bible, it is obvious that God believes we can do something important regardless of what we've accomplished to that point in time. The call of God is based not on what we've done but on the good works that we *will* do.

When we first meet Abraham, all we know is that he is the seventy-five-year-old son of Terah, husband to Sarah (called Sarai at the time), and that he is living with his family and a lot of people and possessions in Haran. But we soon learn that he is a man of faith who is willing to sacrifice when God calls for him to go.

Has God ever called you?

Would you even recognize a call from God if you received one?

Characteristics of a Call

Even though I don't believe that God still speaks to us today in an audible voice (at least I've never had that experience), I do believe he speaks to us through his Word, through the leading of the Holy Spirit, through the wisdom of Holy Spirit-led Christians, through peace, through pain, and through the opening and closing of doors of opportunity.

In Abraham's story we see a couple of the important characteristics of a call from God. These two qualities are consistent with what I've experienced as a

Christian and witnessed in the lives of some of the people with whom I've had the chance to minister.

Unexpected

God seems to like to catch us off guard. He likes surprises.

He likes to speak to a prophet through the mouth of a donkey (Numbers 22:30).

He likes to tell an unwed virgin that her next pregnancy test will be positive (Luke 1:35).

He likes to announce the birth of his Son to a bunch of sleeping shepherds by way of a multitude of angels suddenly appearing in the dark night sky (Luke 2:13, 14).

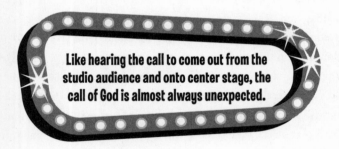

> **Like hearing the call to come out from the studio audience and onto center stage, the call of God is almost always unexpected.**

He likes to walk on water in the middle of the night (John 6:19).

And he likes to tell a childless senior citizen that his descendants will be as numerous as the stars in the heavens (Genesis 15:5).

Like hearing the call to come out from the studio audience and onto center stage, the call of God is almost always unexpected.

You're minding your own business, just driving down the road, when you hear a song on the Christian radio station with a message that immediately compels you to pull over and start weeping because you know its lyrics were written just for you.

Game Show Trivia

Vanna White, letter turner on *The Wheel of Fortune*, was a contestant on *The Price Is Right* on June 18, 1980. She never made it out of contestants' row.

In your daily devotions you read a passage you've read a hundred times before . . . but this time you see something you've never noticed before and you know that it's a message from God.

You're finishing up a time of prayer during which you begged the Lord for help with a personal crisis, when the doorbell rings—it's a friend who just felt led to drop in and see how you're doing.

You sense that God may be calling you to serve on a mission field, but you're five years from retirement and you're afraid that it would be too irresponsible to just quit your job and head with your wife to teach orphans in Haiti. But then—out of the blue—your boss calls you in and tells you that because of the slow economy, the company would like you to take your retirement (with full benefits) early.

Let's not over-spiritualize Abraham's story to the point that we forget that he was just an ordinary guy who was living an ordinary life with his ordinary family in very ordinary Haran . . . when he received a totally unexpected call from God to do something extraordinary.

God's call to Abraham was completely surprising, but—like God's other calls—it was not random.

Motivated by Love

I'm convinced that telemarketing calls are a result of the fall of the human race in the beginning of time.

If Adam and Eve hadn't eaten that forbidden fruit, you and I would be able to finish a meal with our families without having that meal interrupted by a computerized phone call from somewhere in India that's trying to sell us a water purifier, security system, health insurance, or a coupon book—which we think we will use, but we won't. It will just sit in the glove compartment of our car where we'll forget about it until we stumble upon it two years later while searching for our driver's license and registration. I don't know about you, but I sincerely miss the good ol' days when dinner used to be interrupted by an actual person. But I digress.

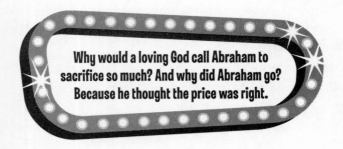

Why would a loving God call Abraham to sacrifice so much? And why did Abraham go? Because he thought the price was right.

Telemarketing phone calls are annoying because they are intrusive and obviously motivated not by love but by a desire to separate us from as much of our money as possible.

Telemarketers only call because they want to take something from us.

God only calls because he wants to give something to us.

He may want to give us a new purpose, a new identity, a new experience, an opportunity to grow, a blessing, or the joy that can only come from serving others in his name.

God is love (1 John 4:8). He creates love. He spreads love. He feels love. He speaks love. He thinks love. He *is* love. So we know that when he interrupts our lives with an unexpected call, his only motive is love.

God loved Abraham and wanted to give him the amazing blessing of being the earthly father of his children, the Israelites. So he called him unexpectedly and said, "Leave your country, your people and your father's household and go to the land I will show you" (Genesis 12:1).

What?!

Isn't God love?

Game Show Trivia

The first showcase offered on *The Price Is Right* was a week's vacation in Acapulco as well as a Kimball organ, a gas range, and floor tiles.

How can God say he loves us and then expect so much from us?

Why would a loving God call Abraham to sacrifice so much? And why did Abraham go? Because he thought the price was right.

He went because he loved God and was willing to pay the price of sacrifice for the benefit of being in the center stage of God's will for his life.

The Cost

I know it sounds redundant and should go without saying, but there is a cost to sacrifice. We humans tend to like the idea of sacrifice without the cost.

We're willing to "amen" a great sermon on loving the poor, but don't expect us to give up our Thanksgiving morning to pass out meals at the soup kitchen downtown.

We can tolerate going to church every week or so, but don't expect us to go into the world as the church. We'll send our checks to missionaries in Africa, but don't expect us to send our children as missionaries to Africa as well.

We'll deny ourselves as long as it means we can still do whatever we want to do, go wherever we want to go, eat whatever we want to eat, buy whatever we want to buy, and not have to miss *The Office* on Thursday nights in order to host a home Bible study.

We'll follow Jesus wherever he wants us to go, as long as it's within an hour's drive of where we grew up.

And we'll take up our crosses as long as they're not the big naily kind that they hang you on, but the kind small enough to hang loosely around our necks and not detract from the fashion statement we're trying to make.

How can we say we love God so much and then expect so little from ourselves?

Game Show Trivia

The *Price Is Right* premiered on NBC on November 26, 1956, replacing *NBC Bandstand*.

Love is sacrifice. And if we love God, then like Abraham we'll be willing to sacrifice everything for him.

Our Comfort

We invest heavily in our own comfort. We want comfortable cars, comfortable beds, comfortable chairs, comfortable shoes, comfortable clothing, and comfortable toilet paper. For too many people comfort is a god to whom they seem willing to sacrifice almost anything—including money, reputation, health, and marriage vows.

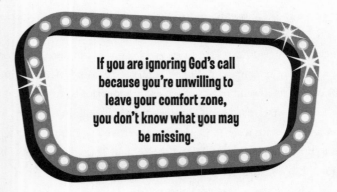

If you are ignoring God's call because you're unwilling to leave your comfort zone, you don't know what you may be missing.

It's relaxing to watch TV for countless hours while your children grow up around you, but it stinks to finally climb out of your La-Z-Boy and find that your kids aren't around anymore.

It feels good to eat too much and exercise too little for most of your life, but dying young is a bummer.

Game Show Trivia

Actress Meg Ryan, then featured in the daytime serial *As the World Turns*, appeared on *The Price Is Right* in 1983 as part of a showcase skit.

And it feels good to sit comfortably on the couch totally uninvolved with the world, while getting up is a real pain.

Comfort without God is an illusion.

If Abraham had ignored God's call—choosing to live comfortably in Haran for the rest of his life—he and his descendants would have missed the true comfort that could only be found in Canaan.

If you are ignoring God's call because you're unwilling to leave your comfort zone, you don't know what you may be missing.

John Muir didn't want to miss anything. He lived in the late 1800s as an explorer of the western United States. According to historian Edwin Teale, in December 1874 John visited a friend who had a cabin on the Yuba River in the Sierra Mountains. During his visit a fierce storm hit the mountains, and the two men retreated to the cabin for a warm fire, a cup of tea, and safety. But without explanation Muir left the cabin, climbed the highest ridge, and pulled himself up to the top of a Douglas fir tree. When asked why he did this, he told his companion that he wanted to experience the storm from the best perch. He could have paid a high price for riding out a storm on top of a tree while holding on for dear life, but it was a price he was willing to pay—he sacrificed his comfort for a more meaningful experience.

Don't be a mere spectator to life, preferring creature comforts to Creator confrontations. But answering God's call to go sacrifice may cost us more than our comfort.

Our Agendas

It appears that Abraham had a pretty good plan in effect for his life. It was a plan that is not too different from our own: get married, settle down, take care of the family, and live a respectable life in a nice town. His agenda may have once included raising a family, but due to his wife's infertility and their old age, having a child together was no longer on his agenda. (Of course, he did try to modify the agenda by having a son with Hagar, but that's another story.) Overall, his life seemed to be going pretty well. He and Sarah had accumulated both servants and possessions, which moved with them when God called them to give up their agenda for his.

Life was good. But God wanted their lives to be *great*, so he called them to sacrifice their agenda for his—which they did—and their lives became legendary. God blessed them with a great nation, a great name, great blessings, and a great son—all because they were willing to go, to sacrifice their agenda for God's.

What is your agenda for your life?

Work hard? Get rich? Live comfortably? Raise a family? Watch TV? Surf the Net? Retire early? Die late?

And how's that working for you?

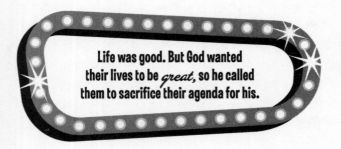

Life was good. But God wanted their lives to be *great*, so he called them to sacrifice their agenda for his.

My friend Jack's plan for his life was working just fine. He was twenty years old and in between rock band gigs. Then God called to him through some sock puppets and a visiting youth minister named Jim, who was doing the children's program at a local revival.

When Jim asked Jack to help with the nightly puppet show, Jack agreed. He had been just hanging out at home (well, his parents' home), so he was open to anything that might be a distraction—even sock puppets. Jack went to the revival, only expecting to sit behind a curtain with a puppet perched on his raised arm, his hand moving the puppet's mouth to silly songs about God. But what he encountered was a humble minister with a life-changing message. Jim took an interest in Jack and came to see him one day to study the Bible. Eventually, Jack embraced the message, gave his life to Christ, and was baptized.

Jack's agenda changed forever.

Instead of pursuing a career as a face-painting rock 'n' roll star, Jack enrolled in a small Bible college in central Florida and began a career as a Bible-believing minister. My friend Jack has been a faithful minister of the Lord for almost thirty years and is currently a professor at the same college where his spiritual journey began.

Jack's life was changed forever when he answered God's call and sacrificed everything—including his agenda—to leave the studio audience and join God on center stage.

What about you? Are you willing to pay the price?

God has big plans for your life. But like Abraham, Sarah, and Jack, it may cost you your comfort and your agenda. You may think the price is too high. Many have.

Or you may think the price is right. If so, listen closely. I think I hear God calling your name.

Can you hear him?

Don't just sit there! He's waiting for you on center stage.

Truth or Consequences

For individual or group study

For Personal Study and Reflection

List your top five favorite possessions. Now to the side of each item write how much that item cost you when you sacrificed to get it. Reflect on why you thought the price was right at the time. Do you still think the price was right? If not, reflect on why not.

1.

2.

3.

4.

5.

For Group Study and Discussion

(Items needed: paper and pens, prize) Pass out paper and pens. Set up a game of The Price Is Right for your group. Purchase a new item and display it in the center of the group. Ask each individual to try to guess the price of the item. The person who comes closest to the actual retail price, without going over, wins the prize. (You may want to draw numbers to determine the guessing order.)

Truth

Read Genesis 12:1-5.

1. Our rules say that we must accomplish a lot of important things before we get called to do something important. Based on what we see in the Bible, it is obvious that God believes we can do something important regardless of what we've accomplished to that point in time. The call of God is based not on what we've done but on the good works that we will *do.*

Can you think of a time when you were called to do something important because of what you had accomplished up to that time? Did you feel qualified for the opportunity? Why or why not? Share or reflect on a time when God called you to do something important. Describe that experience. What did you learn about yourself? What did you learn about God?

2. God seems to like to catch us off guard. He likes surprises.

Share or reflect on a time when you were truly surprised. What was the best part of that experience? Consider a time when God surprised you. Why were you surprised? Did that event change you in any way? How?

3. One look at our bank statements, and we see a clear statement about what we value.

(PERSONAL STUDY: Review your bank statement before answering these questions. GROUP STUDY PARTICIPANTS: Be as honest as you are comfortable being with your small group.) If we were to look at your bank statement right now, what would that statement say about you? Are you pleased with what it says? What would you like your bank statement to say about you? If you're not happy with what your bank statement indicates about you, what is one thing you can do this week to make a positive change?

Consequences

Share or reflect on one thing you learned in this chapter about:

• yourself

• God

How will you use the lessons from this chapter to bring about positive consequences in the lives of the people in your world? Be specific.

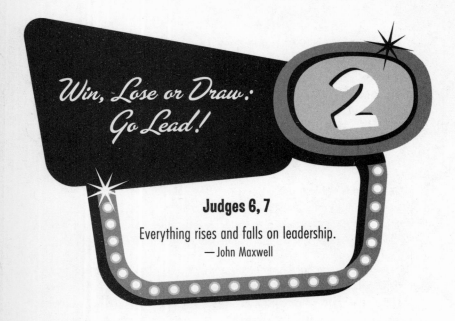

2

Win, Lose or Draw: Go Lead!

Judges 6, 7

Everything rises and falls on leadership.
—John Maxwell

One of the keys to victory on the game show *Win, Lose or Draw* is discernment. If you want to have any chance of winning, you must have at least one team member who has the ability to see substance in the scribbles. Of course, vision is important on *Win, Lose or Draw.* Obviously! One has to be able to see the pad of paper. But discernment—being able to figure out what the artist is drawing—is the key to victory.

The shape of a man's face is drawn on the large pad of paper.

"Richard Nixon!"

The artist rounds the face out.

"Winston Churchill!"

"A basketball!"

"A basketball? Don't forget . . . the category is famous people," the host reminds the artist's teammates.

Quickly the artist adds a beard. One of his teammates scoots to the edge of his seat, yelling, "Moses!"

The other teammate stands up and confidently shouts, "Gandalf!"

"No!" the artist exclaims in a moment of exasperation.

The picture is still unclear.

What should I draw? Think. Think! How can I help them see it? the artist wonders to himself until his frantic thoughts are interrupted by the host.

"Five seconds!"

"I know!" he shouts, as he quickly amends the picture by adding a top hat to the bearded ball.

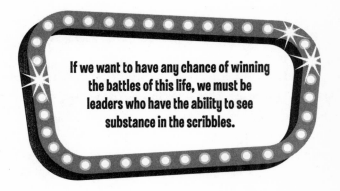

> **If we want to have any chance of winning the battles of this life, we must be leaders who have the ability to see substance in the scribbles.**

And then, a discerning team member sees something familiar in the obscure shapes.

Clarity.

"I know who that is! It's Abraham Lincoln!!"

"That's it!" the host announces.

The audience cheers. The artist and his teammates embrace. Discernment = victory.

One of the keys to victory in life is discernment. One of the lessons we'll see in this chapter is that if we want to have any chance of winning the battles of this life, we must be leaders who have the ability to see substance in the scribbles.

Of course, vision is important for leaders. Obviously! For a leader to see that God is at work is one thing, but when a leader has discernment—the ability to recognize that what God is doing means something—he has the key to victory.

I know, I know. I can hear you: "I'm not a leader. I'm just a ________." (Go ahead. Insert a descriptive title that you think disqualifies you from being considered a true leader—like farmer, soldier, homemaker, administrative assistant, student . . .)

No need to make it complicated. A leader is a person who leads.

Do you lead a staff of a hundred employees in your job? Then you're a leader.

Do you lead your son's baseball team or your daughter's Brownie troop? Then you're a leader.

Do you lead a Sunday school class at church? Then you're a leader.

Do you lead a women's Bible study in your living room on Thursday evenings? Then you're a leader.

Do you lead your friends to more hopeful places when you find them wandering on paths of confusion? Then you're a leader.

Do you lead a subcommittee for your homeowners' association? Then you're a leader.

Are you a parent with a child, a grandparent with grandchildren, an aunt or an uncle, or anyone that anyone could ever be influenced by? Then you're a leader.

Does anyone ever follow you anywhere? Then you're a leader.

Don't get me wrong. There are Leaders and there are leaders. Some people have the God-given ability to lead, so they lead in almost every situation in

Game Show Trivia

***Win, Lose or Draw* was an American television game show that aired from 1987 to 1990 on syndication and NBC.**

which they find themselves. I praise God for men and women like that, but I also praise God for people who may not be Leaders with a capital *L*, but who fearlessly lead when they have to.

So not everyone is a leader all the time, but everyone is a leader at some time or another. You need to be ready when your sometime comes and God calls out to you: "Go lead!"

Ready or Not

Gideon wasn't quite ready when God called him to lead. When we first meet Gideon, he's a little overwhelmed by what he's seeing in the world around him. And who can blame him? It was a difficult time during which to live—and lead.

Gideon's story begins with this ominous assessment of the situation: "Again the Israelites did evil in the eyes of the LORD" (Judges 6:1). This didn't please the Lord, so he allowed the Midianites to oppress the Israelites for seven years. This oppression was so bad that the Israelites were living in mountain clefts, caves, and strongholds in Canaan. During this time the Midianites, Amalekites, and other terrorists invaded their land, killing and destroying everything in their path. The Israelites called out to the Lord for help (v. 6), so he called out for Gideon.

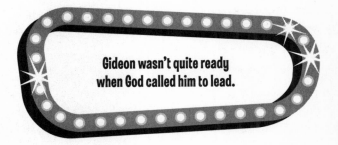

Gideon wasn't quite ready when God called him to lead.

The Lord sent an angel to Gideon, who at the time was threshing wheat in a winepress to keep from being caught by the Midianites. Gideon was hiding. He was afraid. At this particular moment he was what my five-year-old son

Game Show Trivia

One of the original producers of *Win, Lose or Draw* was Burt Reynolds. The original set was modeled after Burt's living room.

would call a scaredy-cat. He was being anything but brave, but the angel of the Lord called Gideon a "mighty warrior" (v. 12).

When God looks at us, he doesn't see scribbles; he sees substance. He sees what we can become even when what we *are* is a mess. When God looked at Gideon he saw a warrior.

When Gideon looked at the situation, he saw a mess. Gideon—sounding more like a worrier than a warrior—asked, "If the Lord is with us, why has all this happened to us? Where are all his wonders that our fathers told us about when they said, 'Did not the Lord bring us up out of Egypt?' But now the Lord has abandoned us and put us into the hand of Midian" (v. 13).

To this the Lord replied, "Go in the strength you have and save Israel out of Midian's hand. Am I not sending you?" (v. 14).

God wanted Gideon to go lead. It was time for him to move from the studio audience to center stage. God was standing at the pad of paper with a marker in his hand, and he was drawing a picture for Gideon. A picture of strength. A picture of deliverance. A picture of hope. A picture of an ordinary man doing extraordinary things. But Gideon still couldn't see it because at this point he wasn't being very discerning.

All he could see was his weakness.

"But Lord . . ."

How annoying it must be for God to hear those two words. As a parent, I know it's annoying to hear such talk, because it's the first ingredient in a long list of things that yield disobedience.

"Son, I need you to make your bed."

"But Dad . . ."

"Sweetie, I need you to pick up your dolls."

"But Dad . . ."

Game Show Trivia

Win, Lose or Draw **was based on the board game Pictionary.**

"Sugar, I need you to get off the computer and start your homework."

"But Dad . . ."

Does any of this sound familiar to you? I know it sounds familiar to God.

"Moses, I need you to go to Pharaoh and bring my people the Israelites out of Egypt."

"But Lord, who am I?" (see Exodus 3:10, 11).

"Jeremiah, I need you go and be my prophet to the nations."

"But Lord, I do not know how to speak; I am only a youth" (see Jeremiah 1:5, 6).

"Jonah, I need you to go to Nineveh."

And Jonah's actions said, "But Lord, I'd rather not" (see Jonah 1:1-3).

God wasn't just doodling on a pad of paper. He had a plan, and Gideon was a huge part of it. So God told Gideon to go. But Gideon, who couldn't make any sense of what God was doing, replied, "But Lord, . . . how can I save Israel? My clan is the weakest in Manasseh, and I am the least in my family" (Judges 6:15).

Gideon's response to God's command reveals the first of a couple of things that can keep leaders from making sense of God's scribbles and accepting God's call to go lead.

A Flawed View of Ourselves

Recently I read about a man who auctioned his life—his house and all its contents, his car, his job, and his friends—on the Internet.[1] The winning bidder purchased Ian Usher for almost $384,000, but Ian was disappointed. He was hoping for more.

Would you have been disappointed too, or are you convinced that you're worthless?

If so, you're wrong. God would pay . . . no, God has *already* paid a high price for your life. He thinks you're priceless.

Gideon didn't think he was worth a dime, but God thought Gideon was invaluable.

God had already made it clear that when he looked at Gideon, he saw the image of a man who was more than qualified for the task. He saw a "mighty warrior" through whom he could defeat the Midianites. He wasn't asking Gideon to be someone else or to do something that he wasn't gifted to do. He just wanted Gideon to go in the strength he had (v.14). But Gideon's view of himself was so flawed, he couldn't make any sense of God's good opinion of him. All he could see was a man who was *less than*. His clan was *less than* all the other clans in Manasseh. He was *less than* all the other members of his family (v. 15).

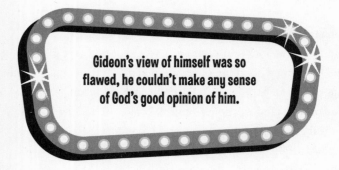

Gideon's view of himself was so flawed, he couldn't make any sense of God's good opinion of him.

Thinking of ourselves humbly is godly; thinking of ourselves as *less than* is ungodly. We were made "in the image of God" (Genesis 1:27). We are "God's workmanship" (Ephesians 2:10). This is how God sees us. I believe that to see ourselves as less than how God's sees us is wrong. We need to fight against *less than* living, *less than* speaking, *less than* singing, serving, thinking, and seeing.

Our God is a *more than* God!

The prophet Elisha testified to this truth when he said, "Don't be afraid. . . . Those who are with us are *more than* those who are with them" (2 Kings 6:16, emphasis added).

This truth was in the promise God spoke to his people through Ezekiel: "I will increase the number of men and animals upon you, and they will be fruitful and become numerous. I will settle people on you as in the past and will make you prosper *more than* before" (Ezekiel 36:11, emphasis added).

And this same truth Paul confirmed to the Christians in Ephesus when he wrote, "Now to him who is able to do immeasurably *more than* all we ask or imagine, according to his power that is at work within us" (Ephesians 3:20, emphasis added).

We have a *more than* God. And when he is with us—who can be against us? But Gideon wasn't seeing this truth clearly because he had a flawed view of himself that had been shaped by the destructive force of overwhelming trials.

Trials don't play well with others. Trials like to punch us in the gut, knock the wind out of our lungs, take all of our lunch money, and shoot our eyes out—blinding us to who we really are.

Christ's brother James teaches us in his letter that trials can build our character (James 1:2-4), but life teaches us that trials can also break our spirits.

One day a group of scientists conducted a simple experiment to study the behavior of monkeys. Five monkeys were placed in a cage with a ladder set up in the middle of the cage. A bunch of bananas was tied to the top of the ladder. The moment the monkeys saw the bananas on top, they tried to climb up the ladder and grab the bananas. When any monkey tried going up the ladder, the scientists showered that monkey with freezing cold water. This happened again and again until all the monkeys in the cage were cold, wet, discouraged, and still banana-less. Eventually, the monkeys stopped going for the bananas. They had given up.

Game Show Trivia

In 1987 the Milton Bradley Company created a board game based on the TV show.

The scientists then took the test a step further by introducing new monkeys into the cage. When the new monkeys saw the bananas, the temptation was too great. They immediately tried to climb the ladder to get to them; but when they did so, the old monkeys grabbed them and held them back.

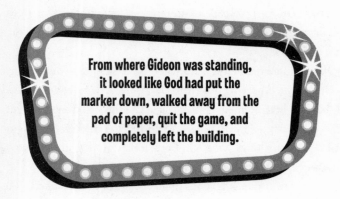

From where Gideon was standing, it looked like God had put the marker down, walked away from the pad of paper, quit the game, and completely left the building.

No cold water was being sprayed, yet the old monkeys kept the new monkeys from reaching the prize because of their own past experience. Going ahead with the experiment, the scientists kept replacing old monkeys with new ones. And every time, the oldest monkeys in the cage would keep the newest monkeys from reaching the bananas at the top of the ladder.

Eventually the cage was full of monkeys who had never received a cold shower, yet who refused to go for the bananas that sat—free for the taking—at the top of the ladder.

That's the power of trials. Trials can make monkeys forget that they are monkeys . . . who love bananas. Trials can break our spirits and make us forget who we really are—mighty warriors who are partnered with God in a victorious cause! Trials can keep us from going.

A Flawed View of God

God had a plan for Gideon's life, so he desperately wanted Gideon to see this truth. But Gideon had been so beaten up by trials that when he looked at his reflection, all he saw was a weakling looking back at him. Looking at the current situation of God's people, he asked, "If the LORD is with us . . . where are all his wonders that our fathers told us about when they said, 'Did not the LORD bring us up out of Egypt?'" (Judges 6:13).

Gideon saw no wonders, no deliverance, no mighty warrior. And that's not all. He was so overwhelmed by the problems in his land that he couldn't even see God. This was Gideon's most serious problem and an example of the second thing that can keep leaders from making sense of God's scribbles and accepting God's call to go lead.

Our view of God impacts how we interact with him and determines whether or not we will go when he tells us to go.

If we view him as a jolly old man with a long white beard, sitting in front of a pile of gifts, we won't want to go and risk missing opening all the presents that we know he is going to give us.

If we see him as a large angry man who yells a lot and looks for the tiniest excuse to throw us into Hell, then we'll stay when he says "go" just because we are paralyzed by fear.

If we perceive him as undeserving of respect, then we'll stay when he says "go," convinced that he is in no position to tell us to do anything or go anywhere.

When we encounter Gideon in that winepress, it's obvious that he wasn't prepared to go and lead because he viewed God as an absent father with no concern for his kids. So instead of going, he started questioning.

Misperception #1—God Is Not Present

Gideon first questions God's presence. From where Gideon was standing, it looked like God had put the marker down, walked away from the pad of paper, quit the game, and completely left the building. He asked, "If the LORD is with us, why has all this happened to us?" and then declared as if he knew it as fact: "But now the LORD has abandoned us and put us into the hand of Midian" (v. 13).

Can you relate to Gideon? Have you ever felt that God has deserted you and you're left on your own to face *your* Midianites? If so, then be encouraged

In 1989 the Disney Channel produced a kids' version called *Teen Win, Lose or Draw* hosted by *Family Ties* star Marc Price.

Game Show Trivia

by the words of David: "The LORD is in his holy temple; the LORD is on his heavenly throne. He observes the sons of men; his eyes examine them" (Psalm 11:4). And take heart in the Lord's promise to Gideon, "I will be with you, and you will strike down all the Midianites together" (Judges 6:16).

Gideon heard what the Lord was saying, but he wasn't yet convinced that God was there to stay. So he asked for a sign, and our ever-present Lord obliged.

The Lord had Gideon place goat meat and bread on an altar, which he then proceeded to torch with fire from a rock.

Wow!

That fire burned up more than a dead goat and a loaf of Wonder Bread; it also burned an important message into Gideon's soul, which read, "I am God and I am here!"

Do you believe that God is here?

He is.

We must never forget that fact.

Gideon needed to remember that God was still in the game; he had not walked away from the pad of paper. He was still holding the marker and drawing an image that he knew well. If Gideon would only stay in the game and be patient, it would become even clearer.

Misperception #2—God Is Not Powerful

Gideon also questioned God's power. He now knew that God was there, but he wasn't convinced that God was powerful enough to help him defeat the Midianites. So Gideon asked for another sign—but this time he would set the terms. And once again, our all-powerful Lord obliged.

Game Show Trivia

Bert Convy, host of *Win, Lose or Draw*, was a baseball player for two years in the Philadelphia Phillies organization.

Gideon placed a fleece on the threshing floor and asked God to prove his power by covering the *fleece* with dew while leaving the *ground* dry. God obliged. The next morning the fleece was wet and the ground was dry (vv. 36-38).

Impressed but not convinced, Gideon boldly asked God to do it again. But this time he wanted the *fleece* to be dry and the *ground* to be wet—and that's exactly what God did (vv. 39, 40), proving yet again that his power should never be called into question.

Have you ever doubted God's power?

I heard a story about a fellow who slid his car off a road and ended up in a ditch. The motorist walked to a nearby farmhouse and asked the owner if he had a tractor he could borrow to get the truck back on the road.

"Nope, but I got my mule, Blue," said the farmer.

"I doubt a mule is strong enough to pull my truck out."

"You don't know Blue," said the mule's proud owner. So Blue was hitched to the truck. "Pull, Blue!" The truck didn't move. And the farmer then called out, "Pull, Elmer!" The truck moved a little. Then the farmer yelled, "Pull, Biscuit!" and the truck was free.

"Thank you so much," said the truck owner. "But I have a question. You called your mule by three different names. How is that?"

"Simple," said the farmer. "Blue is blind. And if he thought he was the only one pulling, your truck would still be in the ditch!"

We must remember—when we're trying to pull elements of our life out of a ditch—that we're not the only ones pulling.

God is powerful, and he wants us out of that ditch more than we can ever know.

At this point in this story, Gideon finally stopped testing God. God resumed his testing of Gideon by picking up the marker again, approaching the pad of paper, and drawing another cryptic picture of what he wanted Gideon to do next—teach the world that God always prevails.

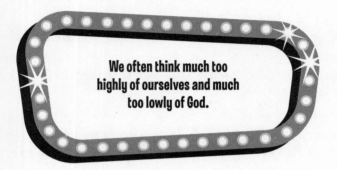

We often think much too highly of ourselves and much too lowly of God.

Misperception #3—God Will Not Prevail

As the time for battle with the Midianites drew nearer, Gideon seemed to have serious questions about God's ability to actually pull off this victory; so he took it upon himself to give God a little help.

It's been my experience that we often think much too highly of ourselves and much too lowly of God.

Actor George Reeves played Superman on the popular 1950s TV program *The Adventures of Superman*. His role required him to make occasional public appearances in his Superman costume. It was not uncommon for Reeves to be poked, punched, or kicked while dressed as the Man of Steel; people wanted to see if he really was invincible.[2]

One famous story about George Reeves has circulated for years. As the legend goes, once when Reeves appeared to speak at a department store wearing the Superman costume, a boy who had taken his father's gun almost shot Reeves.[3] The boy explained that he wanted to watch the bullets bounce off Superman. Luckily, the situation was apparently averted, and thereafter Reeves continued to speak to groups of children, only without the Superman costume. According to people who should know, this story is most likely not true, but simply made up by Reeves so that he wouldn't have to wear the costume at public appearances. Either way, all I can say is, "Good thinking, George!"

He understood how dangerous it is for a human to give the appearance that he's invincible.

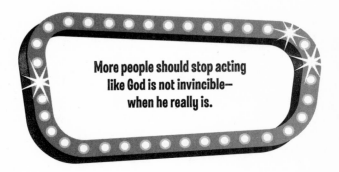

> **More people should stop acting like God is not invincible—when he really is.**

I think more people should follow George Reeves's example and stop acting like they are invincible when they aren't, and more people should stop acting like God is not invincible—when he really is.

God is invincible. He never loses. He always prevails. This was an important lesson for Gideon and the Midianites to learn and for us to remember.

Gideon was doing all he could to help God prevail, but God was drawing up a better plan—a plan that, when clearly seen, would reveal who truly had the power to save Israel.

Making Sense of God's Scribbles

Gideon executed his plan by assembling an army of thirty-two thousand men and setting up camp just south of the Midianites. The Lord took a quick head count and told Gideon that he had too many men for the battle. God knew that if they won with this many men, they would take the glory for the victory and not give the glory to him. So he commanded that anyone who was trembling with fear should go home. Twenty-two thousand men left, leaving Gideon with only ten thousand soldiers. But the Lord told Gideon that number was still too many.

God had Gideon take the men down to a body of water for a drink. He told Gideon that those who knelt down to drink needed to leave, but that those who brought their hands to their mouths and then lapped the water like a dog could stay. God wanted to face the Midianites with men who were perceptive, men who paid attention to what was going on around them, men who kept their heads up—prepared for a possible attack. This last sifting left only three hundred men.

The Lord did one more head count and pronounced that he would indeed prevail, saying, "With the three hundred men that lapped I will save you and give the Midianites into your hands" (Judges 7:7). With this, God sent Gideon and his servant to the Midianite camp for one last round of Win, Lose or Draw.

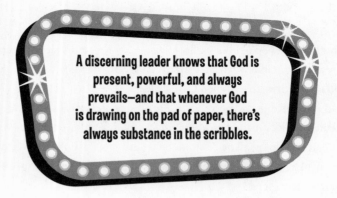

A discerning leader knows that God is present, powerful, and always prevails—and that whenever God is drawing on the pad of paper, there's always substance in the scribbles.

Gideon arrived at the Midianite camp and found an overcrowded campground. The "Midianites, the Amalekites and all the other eastern peoples had settled in the valley, thick as locusts" (v. 12). But just when it seemed that Gideon would—in the face of this enormous army—lose sight of what God had been trying to teach him, God once again picked up the marker, approached the pad of paper, and started to draw a picture. Through a dream that God gave to a Midianite soldier, God drew a picture for Gideon that looked a lot like a round loaf of barley bread rolling through—and crushing—the Midianite camp (v. 13). Then through an interpretation of that dream by a friend of the

Midianite soldier, God drew another picture that was a little clearer—a picture of Gideon's sword.

Suddenly Gideon, a discerning leader, saw something familiar in the obscure shapes.

Clarity.

Gideon discerned the substance in the scribbling so unmistakably that he immediately began to worship God. The image made sense to him. So he returned to the camp and announced what he had clearly seen on God's pad of paper: "Get up! The Lord has given the Midianite camp into your hands" (v. 15).

Read the remainder of Judges 7 to see the outcome—one of cinematic proportions. I'd love to see what Hollywood director Steven Spielberg or Peter Jackson could do with this incredible battle on the silver screen. Gideon gave each man a trumpet and a jar with a torch inside and told them to follow him. The men surrounded the camp, blew their trumpets, broke the jars, grabbed their torches, and shouted, "A sword for the Lord and for Gideon!" (v. 20).

The Midianites scattered in a panic, and the Israelites blew their trumpets again. Then the Lord did something remarkable—he caused the Midianites to turn on each other with their swords. The Midianites fled from southeast of the Sea of Galilee down the Jordan and were trapped when the Ephraimites joined the battle just north of the Dead Sea. The victory was decisive and complete . . . which should be no surprise to any discerning follower of God.

A discerning leader knows that God is present, powerful, and always prevails—and that whenever God is drawing on the pad of paper, there's always substance in the scribbles. I love verse 17: "Watch me," [Gideon] told them. "Follow my lead. When I get to the edge of the camp, do exactly as I do."

Gideon led by example.

You do the same.

Go lead!

Reach for those bananas!

Trust that God knows what he's drawing in this Win, Lose or Draw game and that there's substance in the scribbles you see before you.

Go!

Keep watching, keep asking for discernment, and don't be surprised when—one day in the near future—a discerning Christian friend sees something familiar while observing your life and declares with clarity, "I know who you are! You're a mighty warrior!"

Truth or Consequences

For individual or group study

For Personal Study and Reflection

Secure a copy of today's newspaper, or your favorite magazine, and tear out the pictures of every person you consider to be a great leader. Reflect on how you and these people are similar and how you are different. Now consider how these leaders compare with Gideon in the Bible. Finally, reflect on how you and Gideon are similar and how you are different.

For Group Study and Discussion

(Items needed: paper and pencil) As you begin your study, have each person name the greatest leader they've ever met and share what made this person a great leader. Be specific. Share how this leader impacted the lives of the people in his/her world. Have everyone in the group tell one area in which they are leaders and how this impacts the lives of the people in their world.

Truth

Read Judges 6:14-16.

1. *Gideon wasn't quite ready when God called him to lead. When we first meet Gideon, he's a little overwhelmed by what he's seeing in the world around him. And who can blame him? It was a difficult time during which to live—and lead.*

Consider a time when you were called on to lead. Share or reflect on some of the feelings you encountered during this experience. What did you learn about yourself on this occasion? What did you learn about others? What did you learn about God?

2. When God looks at us, he doesn't see scribbles; he sees substance. He sees what we can become even when what we are is a mess.
Using the paper and pencil, draw a picture that represents what you think God sees when he looks at you right now. Is there anything you'd like to change about this picture? If so, what? If your neighbors were to draw this picture, would it be different from the one you've drawn? What if a family member drew it? your coworkers? What is one thing of substance in your life right now?

3. Trials don't play well with others. Trials like to punch us in the gut, knock the wind out of our lungs, take all of our lunch money, and shoot our eyes out—blinding us to who we really are.
Share or list the top three trials you are facing right now. What are some of the biggest lessons you are learning about life as you face these trials? What have you learned about yourself from facing these trials? What have you learned about God?

4. Our view of God impacts how we interact with him.
Take a few moments and think about God. Draw an image to represent the main characteristic you picture when you think about God. What does this image say about your relationship with him? What does the image say about you?

Consequences

Share or reflect on one thing you learned in this chapter about:

- yourself

- God

How will you use the lessons from this chapter to bring about positive consequences in the lives of the people in your world? Be specific.

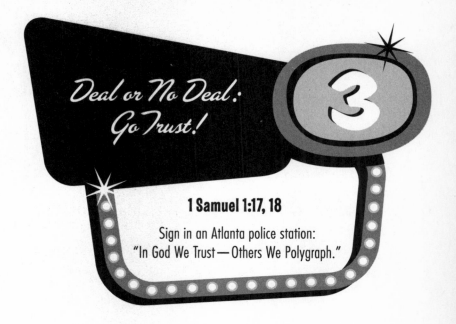

3

Deal or No Deal: Go Trust!

1 Samuel 1:17, 18

Sign in an Atlanta police station:
"In God We Trust—Others We Polygraph."

Trust is easier said than done.

Tracee Jones, a contestant on the hit game show *Deal or No Deal*, told host Howie Mandel that she knew that the case she had picked—case #12—contained the $1 million.[1] But as the game progressed her faith was tested. Jones, a women's basketball head coach at Tennessee State University, was doing pretty well after a bad start. As the game was winding down, the banker offered her $130,000, but she turned it down.

She trusted that the $1 million was in her case, so she played on, opening two more cases.

"Case #21," Tracee said cautiously.

When case #21 was opened, it revealed $100,000. The studio audience groaned, knowing that this would bring the banker's offer down. Next she picked case #4, revealing $10, and the crowd went crazy.

At this point the banker called down to Howie to make Tracee another offer for her case.

The total amount of all the cash awards in the twenty-six briefcases adds up to $3,418,416.01.

Game Show Trivia

"How lucky do you feel?" Howie asked Tracee as he revealed that the banker was offering her $189,000 for her case.

"No deal!" Tracee shouted, as she decided to play on, choosing case #24, which contained one penny!

Now the banker's offered increased to $265,000, and the studio audience went crazy once again.

Tracee trusted that her case contained $1 million. But tempted by such a large sum of money, Tracee decided that she would take the deal—and went home with about $185,000 after taxes.

Trust is easier said than done.

My oldest daughter is on a "trust fall" kick. Periodically she just walks up to me, turns around, and says, "Catch me" as she falls back into my arms.

"Ashton!" I yell, terrified that I'll drop her. "You have to give me some sort of warning!"

"But Dad, I know you'll catch me."

She may know it, but I don't. I'd never forgive myself if I dropped my daughter. I've been known to drop things every once in a while, but she still trusts me.

I wish I still had her kind of faith in people. I wish I had that kind of faith in God. Trust in God is easier said than done.

A young man at a camp meeting was asked just before the Sunday morning service if he would preach. As hundreds of people began gathering on the grounds, the young man panicked and ran into the older preacher's tent. "What shall I do, Preacher John?" he implored. "They've asked me to preach, but I don't have any sermon."

"Trust the Lord, young man," the preacher advised with great dignity. "Just trust the Lord." Then the preacher marched out of his tent. Frustrated, the young man picked up the preacher's Bible and flipped through it, hoping to find an inspiring verse. Instead, he found some typewritten sermon notes he liked very much. He took the preacher's Bible and notes and went to the service. The young minister amazed everyone with his sermon, and the people crowded around him after the service. Suddenly, the preacher pushed his way through the crowd.

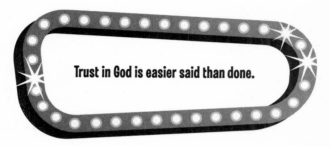

Trust in God is easier said than done.

"Young man," the preacher thundered, "you preached the sermon I was going to preach tonight! Now what am I going to do?"

"Trust the Lord, Preacher John," the young man replied. "Just trust the Lord."

It's easy to just trust the Lord when you have a sermon in hand, a check in hand, a solid job in hand, a happy family in hand, perfect health in hand, or a clear path for your life in hand. It's much harder to trust the Lord when you're broke, unemployed, going through a messy divorce, terminal, clueless about where to go and what to do next, or sermon-less before an eager congregation.

Easy and Difficult

Trust is easy. It's just an awareness that everything is going to be OK because God loves us and is still on his throne.

Trust is difficult. It requires seeing light in darkness, a way over, a path through, an end at the beginning of a painful journey, blue sky during a raging storm, and peace in the midst of a frightening war and unbelievable carnage. Trust is messy, bloody, smelly, bitter, wrenching, terrifying, and often soaked with tears. But you wouldn't know this by the way we Christians use the word.

Game Show Trivia

The least amount won was $1, which happened on the Sunday, May 6, 2007 episode.

We throw the word *trust* around so flippantly—like it's the panacea for every trial.

To a woman who recently had her second miscarriage, we say, "Just trust the Lord."

To the couple who's having a hard time making ends meet, we say, "Just trust the Lord."

To the alcoholic who is trying to maintain sobriety, we say, "Just trust the Lord."

To the young man who must find yet another job, we say, "Just trust the Lord."

To the child whose father died of a massive heart attack, we say, "Just trust the Lord."

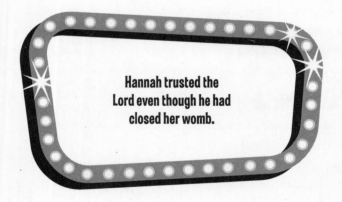

Hannah trusted the Lord even though he had closed her womb.

To the wife who found out that her pastor husband is having an affair with her best friend, we say, "Just trust the Lord."

Game Show Trivia

According to host Howie Mandell, the models often faint from standing at attention for so long.

Yes, God is good. God is faithful. God is powerful. God is love. God is.

And we should trust him. But I believe that will be made easier by a better understanding of what biblical trust really looks like.

It looks like building an ark. It looks like putting your son on an altar. It looks like facing a giant. It looks like being stoned to death. It looks like being imprisoned. It looks like a cross.

And it looks like a barren woman weeping bitterly in the Lord's temple year after year, begging God for a child.

Hannah trusted the Lord even though he had closed her womb, allowed her to be repetitively provoked by a rival, and appeared to be ignoring her constant appeals for a son. Her trust wasn't based on past performance, but on the present knowledge that God is not deaf, dumb, or blind to the desires of his children.

I want to trust the Lord like Hannah did. Trusting in the Lord wasn't optional for Hannah; it was the only thing she could do. She didn't just sing about it, study it, discuss her feelings about it, or listen to the preacher talk about it on Sunday mornings. No. She lived it. She breathed it. She cried it.

We can learn so much from Hannah about what it really means to trust the Lord, but in particular we learn two of the keys to maintaining trust in the face of trials.

Persistence

Elkanah and his wives were persistent in worshiping God. Hannah was one of two women married to Elkanah. Elkanah's other wife, Peninnah, had children, but Hannah did not. Year after year Elkanah and his wives went to worship and sacrifice to the Lord at Shiloh. When the day came to make sacrifices to God, Elkanah would give portions of the meat sacrifices to Peninnah and her sons and daughters, but he would give a double portion to Hannah because he loved her and was burdened with her pain.

Peninnah wasn't a very nice person. The Bible tells us that she kept provoking Hannah "in order to irritate her" (1 Samuel 1:6). Peninnah was also persistent. We read, "Whenever Hannah went up to the house of the LORD, [Peninnah] provoked her till she wept and would not eat" (v. 7).

Hannah had had enough, so she decided to be persistent in something herself: prayer.

The Bible records it this way: "In bitterness of soul Hannah wept much and prayed to the LORD" (v. 10).

I have to stop here and ask a question: What keeps you from praying?

Being too busy?

Feeling as if God is not meeting your needs?

Someone in the church hurt your feelings?

You're tired because you had a hard workout at the gym?

Your spouse isn't making you happy anymore?

You're broke and struggling to feed your three kids (but your selfish, childless brother just bought another sports car and a condo in Cancun)?

Do you know what kept Hannah from praying? Nothing.

She was hurt, she was bitter, she was sad, and she was miserable. But she was committed to trusting God—deal or no deal—so she was persistent in telling him exactly what she wanted. "O LORD Almighty," she vowed, "if you will only look upon your servant's misery and remember me, and not forget your servant but give her a son, then I will give him to the LORD for all the days of his life, and no razor will ever be used on his head" (v. 11).

We are often so vague in our prayers, asking for God to "bless us," "help us," "guide us," and "protect us." Which doesn't give God much opportunity to impress us. For example, we can pray, "Lord, please help us," or we *could* pray, "Lord, please help us to find the $1,250 our neighbor needs to pay the deductible for his daughter's surgery." Now that's a Hannah prayer! If you were God, which prayer would you rather answer?

Hannah was very specific in laying out what she wanted from the Lord and what she was going to do when he answered her prayer. She was making him an offer.

1. Give me a son.
2. I will give him to you.
3. No razor will ever be used on his head.

Deal or no deal?

The Lord loves to answer specific prayers, because when he answers a specific prayer, it proves his power. And when he answers a persistent prayer, it proves his devotion to us.

God is devoted to us.

Hannah's prayer was a pledge of allegiance to God.

She wanted him to know that her belief in him was stronger than the bitterness in her soul, so she persisted in her prayer to the point that she looked like she was drunk.

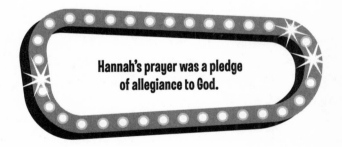

Hannah's prayer was a pledge of allegiance to God.

Because a lot of drunk people talk to themselves, the temple priest Eli thought Hannah was plastered out of her mind. As she prayed, "her lips were moving but her voice was not heard" (v. 13). So Eli said, "How long will you keep on getting drunk? Get rid of your wine" (v. 14).

Hannah wasn't drunk, and she definitely wasn't talking to herself; she was talking to God. She had not been pouring out beer into her cup, she was "pouring out [her] soul to the Lord" (v. 15).

Hannah trusted that her persistence was going to pay off. Observing Hannah is like observing the craftsman whom Jacob Riis referenced when he wrote, "I'd look at one of my stonecutters hammering away at the rock, perhaps a hundred times without as much as a crack showing in it. Yet, at the 101st blow, it would split in two, and I knew it was not that blow that did it, but all that had gone on before."[2] Hannah trusted that if she persisted and kept on hammering away at her problems, they would eventually crumble or become something beautiful.

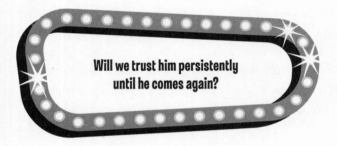

Will we trust him persistently until he comes again?

God responds to persistence. We see it in the Old Testament.

God decided to destroy Sodom and Gomorrah because they had become wicked cities. Abraham was concerned about this plan and begged God to change his mind. Abraham approached God to ask, "Will you sweep away the righteous with the wicked? What if there are fifty righteous people in the city?" (Genesis 18:23, 24).

God agreed. If there were fifty righteous people, he wouldn't destroy the cities. But that wasn't good enough for Abraham, so he asked God if he could lower his number to forty-five. God agreed again, but Abraham wasn't through.

Game Show Trivia

Contestant Michele Falco (who was playing for a top prize of $6 million) currently holds the record of $750,000. She turned down an offer of $880,000.

Abraham persisted in his bargaining and got the Lord to lower the number three more times, to the point of agreeing that if there were ten righteous people in Sodom and Gomorrah, he wouldn't destroy the cities.

There weren't. So the cities were destroyed, but not before teaching us an important lesson about the Lord: he listens to our persistent pleas. He listened to Abraham's, he listened to Hannah's, and he'll listen to yours too.

Jesus, wanting to teach his disciples "that they should always pray and not give up" (Luke 18:1), told them a parable about a widow who kept pleading with a judge for justice against her adversary. The judge refused, but she wouldn't leave him alone. He eventually gave up and gave her what she wanted. Jesus went on to say, "And will not God bring about justice for his chosen ones, who cry out to him day and night? Will he keep putting them off? I tell you, he will see that they get justice, and quickly" (vv. 7, 8). But Jesus didn't end the lesson there. He asked an important question: "When the Son of Man comes, will he find faith on the earth?" (v. 8).

Will he?

Will we trust him persistently until he comes again?

God responded to Hannah's persistence by giving her something beautiful: a son, whom she named Samuel.

Passion

Passion can make trials seem bearable. It is the second key to maintaining trust in the face of a trial, and it is powerful.

My friend Travis is an Ironman. He's completed two Ironman distance triathlon races that required him to swim 2.4 miles, bike 112 miles, and then run a marathon (26.2 miles). You don't accomplish this feat without a lot of hard

Game Show Trivia

The highest amount won in a regular show (jackpot: $1 million) was $402,000 won by Anteia Greer. Her case #21 had only $400.

work. Ten months prior to each race, Travis begins a rigorous training routine before and after work each day. He changes his diet. He changes his sleep patterns. He does whatever he has to do to prepare his body, mind, and soul for a 140.6-mile race—because he is passionate about the sport of triathlon and because he's passionate about finishing the race. His passion pulls him through the pool at five in the morning. His passion drives him down the road on his bike in the heat of the noonday sun. His passion carries him along as he runs the last mile of an eight-mile run, and his passion delivers his weary body across the finish line at the end of a ten-hour race.

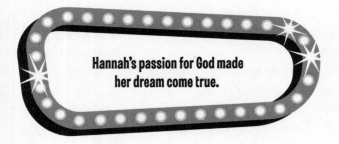

Hannah's passion for God made her dream come true.

Hannah's passion for God helped her to keep trusting him in the midst of terrible trials.

Hannah's passion for God pulled her through Peninnah's provocations. Her passion drove her to her knees in persistent prayer. Her passion carried her soul along as she waged a battle against bitterness. And her passion delivered Samuel back into the loving arms of her Deliverer.

Passion can make dreams come true.

In 1924, Gutzon Borglum dreamed of seeing the images of George Washington, Abraham Lincoln, Thomas Jefferson, and Theodore Roosevelt on the 6,000-foot granite face of Mount Rushmore. He announced to the world, "American history shall march along that skyline." But placing the images of four dead presidents on the side of a mountain is easier said than done, so it was a good thing that Borglum's dream was backed by a passion to do whatever it took to make his vision become a reality. Borglum hired experienced miners to do most of the sculpting, and under his direction—working with

Game Show Trivia

Deal or No Deal **host Howie Mandel reportedly adopted the "fist bump" instead of a traditional handshake as a friendly way to avoid his contestants' germs.**

jackhammers and dynamite—they removed some 400,000 tons of outer rock, cutting with in three inches of the final surface. Over the next fourteen years, as the stonecutters hammered away at the rock, they eventually created something beautiful that stands today as a lasting tribute to the power of Gutzon Borglum's passion.

Hannah's passion for God made her dream come true.

God gave her a son, and she—as she had promised—gave him right back. As soon as Samuel was weaned, Hannah took him to Shiloh where he joined Eli in serving the Lord . . . passionately.

Hannah longed for a son. She passionately prayed for a son. She passionately poured out her soul to the Lord, explaining what she would do if God gave her a son. Then after giving her son back to God, her passion burst forth from her soul as she praised God for making her dreams come true.

She praised God for honoring her and bringing her joy (1 Samuel 2:1).

She praised God for being her "Rock" (v. 2).

She praised God for delivering her (vv. 4-6).

She praised God for providing for her (vv. 7, 8).

She praised God for protecting her (v. 9).

She praised God for giving her strength (v. 10).

I praise God that Hannah was committed to trusting God—deal or no deal—because trust is easier said than done.

Just ask Tracee Jones.

When we left Tracee, she was on her way home from the hit game show *Deal or No Deal* with $185,000—after taxes.

Tracee had made a deal. But before the show ended, Howie wanted her to see what would have happened if she had kept her trust in the case she selected at the beginning of the show. How good a deal had Tracee made?

Howie asked what case she would have chosen if she had said "No deal." She said her next case would have been case #9.

It contained the $500,000.

The banker's offer would have been $231,000—a $34,000 drop.

Howie continued by asking her the next case she would have chosen if she had decided to stay in the game.

She picked case #14, which held $50.

The banker's offer would have been $361,000.

She identified the next case she would have selected: case #26 that held $300.

If she had stayed in the game, the banker would have offered her $500,000 at this point to quit the game.

Finally, Howie opened Tracee's case, case #12, and the audience groaned, because Tracee's case held $1 million.

Ouch!

A few months later Tracee was interviewed about her experience on the show and how it felt to see the $1 million in her case. She said, "I don't feel bad. I always felt like I had $1 million in my case, but I kept thinking, 'But what if I don't?'"[3]

"But what if I don't?" is the question Satan will try to plant in your heart because he knows that trust is easier said than done.

He wants you to sell your birthright.

He wants you to leave the temple barren.

He wants you to stay in the boat.

He wants you to stay in the studio audience.

He wants you to miss Heaven.

He wants you to sell your case . . . because he knows what's inside.

Don't do it.

Be like Hannah. Don't think you aren't holding an eternal treasure.

You are. So just keep trusting—deal or no deal.

Deal?

Truth or Consequences

For individual or group study

For Personal Study and Reflection

Get a $20 bill before starting this time of personal reflection. On the bill locate the phrase *In God we trust*. Now write that phrase below, but personalize it by replacing the word *we* with your name.

List three things that regularly interfere with your trust in God.

1.

2.

3.

Next to each item above, write a promise from God (with a Scripture reference if you know one) that should help remove this interference. Finally, as an act of trust, ask God to whom you should give the $20 bill. Sometime today give your $20 bill to whomever God lays on your heart.

For Group Study and Discussion

Have your group pair up (preferably not with a spouse or a best friend). Have one person from each pair face away from his/her partner. At your command each person facing away will fall backwards into the arms of his/her partner. (You can also do this by having one person fall back into the arms of a group of people if you're afraid someone may actually be dropped.) Once every person has taken a turn, discuss what it felt like to fall backwards, having to trust someone to make the catch.

Truth

Read 1 Samuel 1:1–2:11.

1. I want to trust the Lord like Hannah did. Trusting in the Lord wasn't optional for Hannah; it was the only thing she could do. She didn't just sing about it, study it, discuss her feelings about it, or listen to the preacher talk about it on Sunday mornings. No. She lived it. She breathed it. She cried it.
Share or reflect on a time when you put your trust in God. What were the results? What were some of the biggest spiritual barriers you had to overcome to be faithful to God in that situation?

2. The Lord loves to answer specific prayers, because when he answers a specific prayer, it proves his power. And when he answers a persistent prayer, it proves his devotion to us.
Share or reflect on a time when you prayed a specific prayer and God answered it. What was the prayer? How did God answer it? How did the answer to that prayer impact your life and the lives of people around you?

3. Passion can make dreams come true.
What are some of your biggest passions right now? How are these passions impacting your life? Consider your biggest dream for your life right now. Are the passions you just mentioned a help or a hindrance in making your dream come true?

Consequences

Share or reflect on one thing you learned in this chapter about:

- yourself

- God

How will you use the lessons from this chapter to bring about positive consequences in the lives of the people in your world? Be specific.

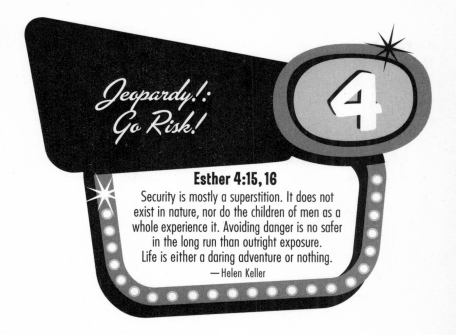

4

Jeopardy!: Go Risk!

Esther 4:15, 16

Security is mostly a superstition. It does not exist in nature, nor do the children of men as a whole experience it. Avoiding danger is no safer in the long run than outright exposure. Life is either a daring adventure or nothing.

—Helen Keller

We weren't designed by God to play it safe.

This is evident in the way we make our entrance into this world. Birth isn't safe; it's a violent, messy process during which we are pushed out of the safety of the womb into a bright, cold, and dangerous world to be completely dependent on others for our survival. Eventually we find our way to the safety of a crib, but that's not the end, because we weren't born to sit in a crib for the rest of our lives either.

At the proper time we are pulled from the safety of the crib and urged to get up and walk. Walking isn't safe at the beginning. Learning to walk is

Game Show Trivia

The first Final Jeopardy category was Famous Quotes, and the answer was "'Good night sweet prince' was originally said to him." The correct answer was "Who is Hamlet?"

a process during which we fall again and again, sometimes getting bruises or even broken bones. But we weren't designed to crawl around on the safety of the ground for the rest of our lives, so our loving parents—wanting more for us—eagerly urge us to take those important first steps.

And then before we know it, we are encouraged to risk even more when we are put on a bicycle on hot, black asphalt, then pushed to breakneck speed and eventually released—with the encouragement to "Keep pedaling!"

Children of wise parents experience countless moments like this, moments when they find themselves in unsafe situations orchestrated by their parents to help them become better, stronger, smarter, braver, humbler, and more mature.

Parents encourage us to try out, knowing we might not be selected.

They encourage us to stand at the plate, knowing that we might strike out.

They encourage us to go to school, knowing that we will be tested.

They encourage us to pray in public, knowing that we may stumble over the words.

They encourage us to build relationships with other people, knowing that we may get our hearts broken.

They encourage us to get a job, knowing that we may get fired.

They encourage us to leave home, knowing that we may get homesick.

They encourage us to get married, knowing that we will face times that are much more "for worse" than "for better."

They encourage us to have children, knowing that those children may disappoint us.

They encourage us to love them, knowing that we will one day bury them.

Game Show Trivia

**The first champion,
Mary Eubanks of North Carolina, won $345.**

They encourage us to follow Jesus, knowing that we will have to take up a cross to do so.

How could loving parents do this? Put their precious little boys and girls at such risk?

How could loving parents *not* do this?

God Is Not Safe

Risk is life; life is risk. A safe life is not just boring; it's ungodly. Your safety may be the Transportation Security Administration's priority, but it's not God's.

God is not safe. We are mistaken when we believe that dwelling in the center of his will for our lives is without risk. In fact, based on what we observe in the lives of our faithful predecessors, the closer we draw to God, the more "at risk" we may find ourselves.

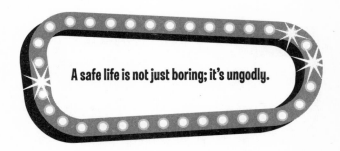

A safe life is not just boring; it's ungodly.

God commanded Abraham to leave the safety of Haran (Genesis 12:1).

God expected Isaac to lie down on an altar (Genesis 22:9).

God's plan for Joseph sent him to a pit and to prison (Genesis 37:24; 39:20).

God sent Moses to risk his life by confronting Pharaoh (Exodus 3:10).

God allowed Shadrach, Meshach, and Abednego to be thrown into a fiery furnace (Daniel 3:19, 20).

Daniel was cast into a lions' den (Daniel 6).

Joseph, Mary, and Jesus had to escape for their lives to Egypt (Matthew 2:13).

John the Baptist was beheaded (Matthew 14:10).

Most of the disciples were martyred for their faith in Christ.

Safety is for wimps and pagans!

And the opposite is risk, which requires faith.

Sitting in the studio audience is safe. You never miss a question, you never lose a dime, and you never have to be in jeopardy in any way. But sitting in the studio audience also guarantees that you're never going to win.

That's why there are people who work very hard to put themselves on *Jeopardy!*

"Alex, I'll take Game Show Trivia for $500."

The answer is, "The number of people who make it onto *Jeopardy!* each season."

"What is five hundred?"

"That's correct."

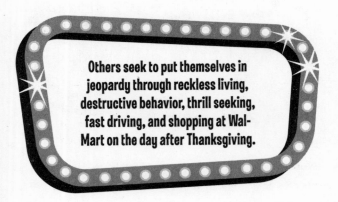

Others seek to put themselves in jeopardy through reckless living, destructive behavior, thrill seeking, fast driving, and shopping at Wal-Mart on the day after Thanksgiving.

Although only five hundred make it, many more want to be on the hit game show *Jeopardy!* Every year, a quarter of a million people apply for an audition to be on the show, either through the station that broadcasts the show in their area or by contacting the show itself. Only fifteen thousand are chosen for the initial screening exam, and only fifteen hundred qualify to become contestants. Then only five hundred actually make it on the air.[1]

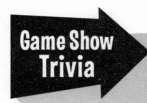

Game Show Trivia

In September 1974, *Jeopardy!* began airing once a week in a nighttime syndicated version.

Others seek to put themselves in jeopardy through reckless living, destructive behavior, thrill seeking, fast driving, and shopping at Wal-Mart on the day after Thanksgiving.

Jake Brown falls into this category. Not the shopping at Wal-Mart on the day after Thanksgiving part, but the thrill-seeking part. He is a professional skateboarder who made headlines in the summer of 2007 during the X Games in Los Angeles.[2] My boys and I were happily watching the skateboarders do tricks off the Big Air Mega Ramp that had been created in the middle of a stadium. The skateboarders were making it all look so easy. We weren't thinking about how risky it was . . . until Jake Brown's run.

As he came up the side of the gigantic quarterpipe, his skateboard flew away from his feet. He lost control and fell more than 40 feet to the flat floor below. Twenty thousand fans, the TV commentators, and my boys and I fell immediately silent, thinking that Jake Brown had just died right before our eyes. I told the boys to look away. It was horrific. This guy had fallen four stories; he'd turned over in the air and landed on his tailbone, with head and limbs hitting soon after.

Amazingly, in a few minutes Jake Brown got up and walked away with only a slight concussion.

He vowed to start skateboarding again as soon as he was completely healthy.

Initially I wondered as I watched the replay of Jake's accident, *Why would anybody choose to do that?*

I'm sure that's what King Xerxes was wondering as he listened to Esther's plea.

Game Show Trivia

The original title for *Jeopardy!* was to be *What's the Question?* but it was changed before the show premiered on NBC.

Becoming Queen

When Queen Esther confronted Xerxes, she wasn't engaging in reckless behavior. She didn't have a death wish; she just wanted to be faithful. But let's back up.

At the time, Xerxes ruled over 127 provinces stretching from India to the upper Nile region (constituting what was then Persia and is modern-day Iran). He was a very wealthy man who enjoyed showing off his amassed treasures. During the third year of his reign, he invited all nobles and officials to a feast where—for 180 days—he displayed all of his glorious wealth.

A week into the festivities, he summoned his wife, Queen Vashti, to the banquet—not to enjoy the festivities but to be a part of the spectacle. He wanted her to put on her crown in order to display her beauty to the crowd. She refused, which enraged Xerxes. After consulting with his experts in the law, he removed Vashti from office and banned her from his presence.

Xerxes issued an edict to bring all of the region's beautiful women into his harem so he could find a replacement for Vashti. One of the women brought into Xerxes' harem was a young Jewish orphan named Esther. Esther had been raised by her cousin Mordecai. Upon Esther's capture, Mordecai warned her not to reveal her nationality and family background, so she kept quiet. Esther was very popular and immediately rose through the ranks of the harem—eventually being chosen by Xerxes to be the new queen.

Soon after her appointment, Mordecai overheard two men conspiring to assassinate Xerxes and got word to Esther so that she could warn the king. Mordecai's report was documented, investigated, and found to be true. The conspirators were captured and executed.

After these events Xerxes promoted a man named Haman to a position of power. Haman was not a good person. He despised Mordecai because he wouldn't kneel down when Haman passed. Haman wanted to kill Mordecai, but decided it would be more effective to kill not only Mordecai, but all Jews. And he convinced Xerxes to order that everyone who disobeyed the king's laws should be killed.

When Mordecai found out about this plan, he got word to Esther and urged her to go into the king's presence to beg for the lives of the Jews.

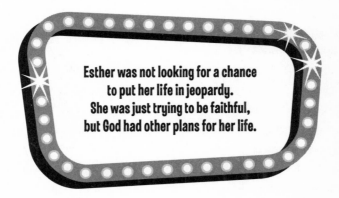

Esther was not looking for a chance to put her life in jeopardy. She was just trying to be faithful, but God had other plans for her life.

Risking Her Life

Answer: "Esther going to Xerxes without being invited into his presence and questioning one of his decrees."

Question: "What is a death sentence?"

Esther was not looking for a chance to put her life in jeopardy. She was just trying to be faithful, but God had other plans for her life. She was playing Jeopardy! whether she wanted to or not.

Esther was scared, but Mordecai—convinced that this young woman, whom he had raised as his own daughter and whom he loved deeply, was being called by God to leave the studio audience and go onto center stage—urged her to trust God, saying, "Do not think that because you are in the king's house you alone of all the Jews will escape. For if you remain silent at this time, relief and deliverance for the Jews will arise from another place, but you and your father's

Game Show Trivia

Before becoming one of America's top game show emcees, Alex Trebek was one of Canada's top television personalities.

family will perish. And who knows that you have come to royal position for such a time as this?" (Esther 4:13, 14).

Esther wasn't a thrill seeker. She wasn't looking for this. She was content being an anonymous face in the studio audience of life. But here she was on center stage with an incredibly important and risky opportunity.

You were not born to play it safe.

You may be in a scary situation—a situation you didn't ask to be in but are in nonetheless. You weren't looking to play Jeopardy! but here you are being called to go risk something for God.

You may feel like God is calling you to go risk your job security by confronting an immoral boss.

You may feel like God is calling you to go risk your position in the PTA by confronting the school board about the sex education curriculum they are proposing.

You may feel like God is calling you to go risk your reputation in the community by publicly opposing the placement of an abortion clinic in your neighborhood.

You may feel like God is calling you to risk your engagement with your fiancé by confronting him about the pornography you found on his computer.

Who knows but that you have been placed in that situation for such a time as this?

We should never take a risk recklessly. There are two important things we can learn from Esther about risk-taking.

Risking for the Right Reason

Answer: "Do you want to see something cool?"

Question: "What are a redneck's last words?"

Game Show Trivia

On the January 19, 1993 broadcast, Air Force Lt. Colonel Daryl Scott of Washington, D.C., became the first player to win the championship with the least amount possible: $1.

Unlike many of us who put our safety at risk because we are being reckless or sinful, Esther's safety was in jeopardy because she was being faithful to God. There was nothing sinful about how she handled this challenge. In fact, when she realized that she had to go and risk her safety for the safety of her people, she called all of the Jews in Susa to a three-day fast, saying, "When this is done, I will go to the king, even though it is against the law. And if I perish, I perish" (Esther 4:16).

God does not expect you to risk your safety recklessly—and it would be reckless to risk anything without first seeking God's will in the matter. We must bathe each decision in prayer. We must enlist the spiritual support of our brothers and sisters in Christ. We must pause to fast lest we move too quickly into a situation that puts our spiritual safety in unnecessary jeopardy.

Think about how Jesus handled the last risky situation of his earthly ministry. Jesus was preparing to take the first steps down a road that would end with the sacrifice of his life, so—before doing anything else—he went to Gethsemane to pray. He asked Peter, James, and John to pray with him. He was preparing to put his life in jeopardy, so he paused and prayed a prayer that we too should pray before risking anything in the name of Jesus: "My Father, if it is not possible for this cup to be taken away unless I drink it, may your will be done" (Matthew 26:42).

Risking for a Higher Purpose

Answer: "Not selfish, but self-sacrificing."

Question: "What was the nature of the risk that Esther took when she appealed to Xerxes?"

When Esther donned her royal robes and stood in front of the king's hall, hoping that he would notice her and invite her in, she was not thinking about herself. She wasn't vying for more attention, more power, or more wealth. In fact, after noticing her and inviting her into his presence, Xerxes offered her up to half of his kingdom (Esther 5:3), and she turned it down—because she wasn't there to get more for herself. Her motives were not selfish. She was risking her life—not for herself but for her people and a higher purpose.

Too many people in our culture put themselves in jeopardy only when it might pay off for them with more pleasure, prestige, or plunder. They'll risk getting a sexually transmitted disease for a few moments of pleasure with a stranger. They'll risk their health—and family—working overtime just to be considered for that corner office. They'll risk their lives on a reality game show for the chance to win a $100,000 grand prize. These actions are not heroic; they're reckless.

There's a difference between being reckless and taking a risk for something that matters. True heroes recognize this; they risk their lives only when it matters.

Wesley Autrey is a true hero. On January 2, 2007, Wesley was preparing to board the subway with his two daughters, when a twenty-year-old stranger, Cameron Hollopeter, began to have a seizure and fell onto the tracks in front of them.[3] A train was barreling toward the man, and Wesley knew that something had to be done.

"I had to make a split decision," Wesley said.

So he made one—and leaped.

Without hesitation, Wesley, a fifty-year-old construction worker, jumped onto the tracks and threw himself on top of the young man. Wesley said the man was still moving violently from the seizure, so he pulled him into the center of the tracks and lay on top of him as the train thundered over the two men. Autrey said there was "maybe" about 2 inches between their bodies and the speeding subway.

Here's a quote from one of the witnesses to this heroic event: "We're looking and we can see the train coming—there's no way the train can stop before this gentleman can get him off the tracks," said Patricia Brown, a social worker to whom Wesley had handed over his daughters before he dived onto the tracks.

"So he covered him with his body and pushed him down to a point where the train wouldn't hit his head and held him . . . while the train came and rolled right over the top of them."

Wesley was not a thrill seeker looking for an adrenaline rush that would make him feel "alive." He was simply a hero making sure that another person stayed alive.

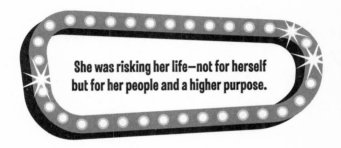

She was risking her life—not for herself but for her people and a higher purpose.

Esther was a true hero too. At great risk to her own life, she stood boldly before Xerxes and Haman and asked, "If I have found favor with you, O king, and if it pleases your majesty, grant me my life—this is my petition. And spare my people—this is my request" (Esther 7:3).

When Xerxes found out that Haman was behind the scheme to kill all the Jews, he had him hanged on the very same gallows that Haman had prepared to hang Mordecai. Mordecai was remembered for having saved Xerxes' life, so Xerxes elevated him to a lofty position. Mordecai's first act was to issue an edict giving the Jews the right to assemble and protect themselves. For the Jews it was "a time of happiness and joy, gladness and honor" (8:16)—all because a simple Jewish girl decided not to play it safe when she found herself unexpectedly playing a game of Jeopardy!

Answer: "A time of happiness and joy, gladness and honor."

Question: "What will happen in the lives of lost and hurting people in this world when Christians decide to stop playing it safe and go risk it all to tell them about the love of Jesus Christ?"

Truth or Consequences

For individual or group study

For Personal Study and Reflection

List three things you could do for God in the next week that would require a risk on your part.

1.

2.

3.

Now circle the one that you *will* do.What are your three biggest fears about accomplishing this task?

1.

2.

3.

Now pray over this list, asking God to help you face your fears faithfully.

For Group Study and Discussion

(Items needed: requested photos) Ask all group members to bring photos from a time when they risked their lives for something. Each member can briefly describe the circumstances and then answer these two questions. Was it worth it? Why or why not?

Truth

Read Esther 4:12-16.

1. We weren't designed by God to play it safe.
Share or reflect on a time when you felt safe. Why did you feel safe in that situation? Share or reflect on a time when you did something risky for God. How did that experience impact your life? How did that experience impact your relationship with God?

2. God is not safe. We are mistaken when we believe that dwelling in the center of his will for our lives is without risk. In fact, based on what we observe in the lives of our faithful predecessors, the closer we draw to God, the more "at risk" we may find ourselves.
Recall an example of someone in the Bible (besides Esther) who was at risk while doing God's will. How did that experience impact that person's life? What do the following Scriptures teach us about why God allows us to be in unsafe situations for his sake?

Romans 5:3-5

Philippians 3:10, 11

James 1:2-4

1 Peter 1:6, 7

3. There's a difference between being reckless and taking a risk for something that matters.
Share or reflect on a time when you did something reckless. How did that experience impact your life? Share or reflect on a time when you took a risk for something that mattered. How did you feel after that experience?

Share or write down one thing that you can do for God in the next month that really matters.

Consequences

Share or reflect on one thing you learned in this chapter about:

- yourself
- God

How will you use the lessons from this chapter to bring about positive consequences in the lives of the people in your world? Be specific.

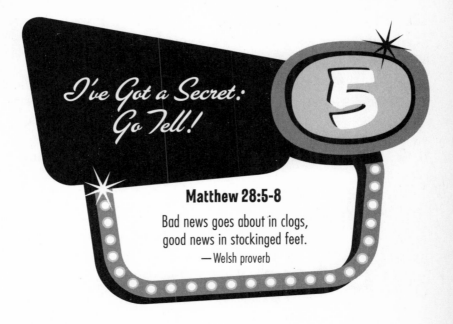

5

I've Got a Secret: Go Tell!

Matthew 28:5-8

Bad news goes about in clogs,
good news in stockinged feet.
—Welsh proverb

Can you keep a secret?

Stephen and Louise couldn't.

"Our son became an astronaut today."

On September 17, 1962—in one of the most interesting segments of game show history—Stephen and Louise Armstrong appeared on *I've Got a Secret* with the secret that their son Neil had just been selected to be an astronaut.[1] Neil was one of nine new men so chosen. What made this appearance especially unique was that host Garry Moore asked Louise an incredible question: "Now, how would you feel, Mrs. Armstrong, if it turned out—of course nobody knows—but if it turns out that your son is the first man to land on the moon? What, how do, how would you feel?" Neil's mom's reply was priceless: "Well, guess I'd just say God bless him and I wish him the best of all good luck." A little less than seven years later, on July 20, 1969, Neil Armstrong became the first man to walk on the moon.

The Armstrongs' secret was so good they couldn't keep it—and understandably so. It was the kind of secret that had to be told.

Not all secrets are the same.

Secrets That Shouldn't Be Told

As an FBI agent, Robert Hanssen was entrusted with some of the biggest military secrets of the United States. In February 2001, Robert Hanssen was arrested and charged with selling American secrets to the KGB in Moscow. He was paid more than $1.4 million for the secrets he shared over a twenty-two-year period. Mr. Hanssen is currently serving a life sentence in Colorado, during which he spends twenty-three hours a day in solitary confinement. His activities have been described as "possibly the worst intelligence disaster in U.S. history."[2] The secrets he shared cost human lives and put the lives of every American in danger.

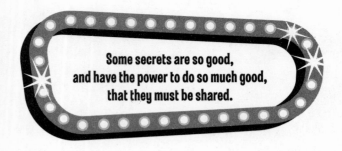

Some secrets are so good, and have the power to do so much good, that they must be shared.

Secrets That Should Be Told

Some secrets are so good, and have the power to do so much good, that they must be shared.

Medical secrets, once revealed, have the power to heal diseases.

Beauty secrets, once revealed, have the power to restore a woman's self-esteem.

Secrets to success, once revealed, have the power to jump-start someone's career.

Financial secrets, once revealed, have the power to build a valuable portfolio.

Weight-loss secrets, once revealed, have the power to transform a body.

Parenting secrets, once revealed, have the power to heal a family.

The secrets to a happy marriage, once revealed, have the power to restore a relationship. (My grandfather Maxey once told me that the secret to a happy marriage was found in two words: "Yes ma'am.")

Dog-training secrets, once revealed, have the power to keep me from giving my dog, Cooper, back to the pound (just kidding, Ashton). My wife is a huge fan of the show *The Dog Whisperer*, hosted by Cesar Millan. She's convinced me that he holds the secret to properly training any dog. I've seen him subdue the most wild and out-of-control dogs without ever saying a word. He never yells at the dogs or hits them. He's learned the secret to becoming the alpha dog in any pack. And the secret is: stay calm and assertive.

There you go.

Here's the problem. My wife and I have allowed this secret to impact our dog training in very different ways. Rhonda has chosen to unleash the power of this secret on her dealings with Cooper, and she has become the alpha dog in Cooper's life. It took several months, but Rhonda—by staying calm and assertive—has complete control over Cooper.

I, on the other hand, have chosen a different approach. I've chosen to do absolutely nothing with the secret Cesar revealed, so Cooper and I continue to have a very frustrating relationship. He jumps on the couch. I tell him to get down. And he looks me in the eye—with a smirk—while he makes himself more comfortable by wrapping my favorite Mexican blanket around his shoulders.

Game Show Trivia

***I've Got a Secret*, one of the most popular and longest-running panel shows, was initially canceled by CBS after thirteen weeks. The network later reversed its decision, and the show remained on the primetime schedule for fifteen years.**

Game Show Trivia

On August 19, 1959, guest Johnny Carson (yes, *that* Johnny Carson!) shot an apple off host Garry Moore's head during the show.

It's really not his fault; it's mine. I know the secret, but I've done nothing with the information.

The Power of Sharing the Right Secrets

God hasn't kept a lot of secrets from us. Sure, he hasn't told us when Christ is coming back again, but—besides that one—he has revealed everything we needed to know at the time we needed to know it.

The Bible is a collection of secrets that weren't meant to be kept forever. It's a revelation of revelations designed to unleash goodness in this world, which is even more amazing in light of the fact that he didn't have to tell us anything. He could have just kept the revelations hidden in the dark—existing, ruling, helping, fixing, and loving this world without ever letting us in on who, or what, was behind the curtain.

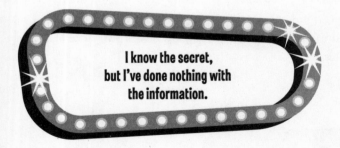

I know the secret, but I've done nothing with the information.

Imagine never knowing whether there is more beyond the sky. Imagine what it would be like to think that we are alone on this planet. Imagine how desperate we would feel in dangerous times if we thought the only power at our disposal was our own.

Game Show Trivia

Boris Karloff (who often portrayed creepy characters in scary movies) was the first guest and presented his secret: "I am afraid of mice."

Some children are afraid of the dark. Sally was one of those children. When she went to bed, she would shout, "Dad, can I have a glass of water?" Her dad would bring it in. A few minutes later, Sally would say, "Dad, can you come and tuck me in again?" Her dad would come and tuck her in. A few minutes later, Sally would say, "Dad, can you come say a prayer with me before I go to sleep?" Her dad would come and say a prayer with her.

One night Sally asked her dad, "If I wake up during the night, afraid of the dark, will you be there for me?"

"Yes, of course I will," her dad replied.

Later on when her dad went to bed, Sally called out from down the hallway, "Dad, are you asleep yet?"

"Sally, it's time to go to sleep!"

"But Dad, if I need some water during the night, will you be there for me?"

"Yes, of course I will," her dad responded, a little exasperated.

"Dad, are you sleeping on your right side or your left?"

"My left . . . now go to sleep."

Then Sally asked her dad one last question. "Dad," she said, "can I ask you one more thing? Is your face turned toward me?"

And with tear-filled eyes, her dad replied, "Yes Sally, my face is turned toward you."

Isn't it comforting to know that there is a God and that his face is always toward us?

He revealed an amazing secret to David: "The eyes of the Lord are on the righteous" (Psalm 34:15).

God has also revealed other amazing secrets to us.

Want to know the secret to having joy in this life? God shared it when through Jesus he told us, "If you obey my commands, you will remain in my love, just as I have obeyed my Father's commands and remain in his love. I have told you this so that my joy may be in you and that your joy may be complete" (John 15:10, 11).

Want to know the secret to having peace? God shared it when through Paul he told us, "Do not be anxious about anything, but in everything, by prayer and petition, with thanksgiving, present your requests to God. And the peace of God, which transcends all understanding, will guard your hearts and your minds in Christ Jesus" (Philippians 4:6, 7).

Want to know the secret to being wealthy beyond your wildest imagination? God shared that secret too, when through Jesus he told us, "Do not store up for yourselves treasures on earth, where moth and rust destroy, and where thieves break in and steal. But store up for yourselves treasures in heaven, where moth and rust do not destroy, and where thieves do not break in and steal" (Matthew 6:19, 20).

Want to know the secret to recognizing true love? God shared it when through Paul he told us, "Love is patient, love is kind. It does not envy, it does not boast, it is not proud. It is not rude, it is not self-seeking, it is not easily angered, it keeps no record of wrongs. Love does not delight in evil but rejoices with the truth. It always protects, always trusts, always hopes, always perseveres. Love never fails" (1 Corinthians 13:4-8).

Want to know the secret to having eternal life? God shared it when he told us, "For God so loved the world that he gave his one and only Son, that whoever believes in him shall not perish but have eternal life" (John 3:16).

Secrets are powerful, so good secrets must be told.

Like the secret God told Mary Magdalene, Mary the mother of James, and Salome on the Sunday morning after Christ's crucifixion when—through an

Game Show Trivia

Former president Ronald Reagan made nine appearances on *I've Got a Secret.*

angel of the Lord—God revealed, "He is not here; he has risen, just as he said" (Matthew 28:6; see Mark 16:1). This was a good secret, too good to be left untold. The angel of the Lord told these women to share it immediately, saying, "Go quickly and tell his disciples" (Matthew 28:7).

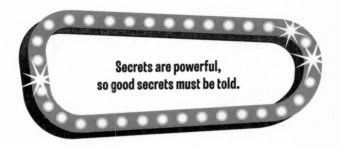

**Secrets are powerful,
so good secrets must be told.**

In the details of this event, there are three secrets that we must reveal as we go and tell people the good news.

"Fears Can Be Overcome."

I find cemeteries to be scary places at night and not much more pleasant during the day. I believe in God, Heaven, "the sweet by and by," the streets of gold, and all other unimaginable beauty of eternal life after death. I believe that when the roll is called up yonder I'll definitely be there, but I'm still not eager to die. Every time I go to a cemetery, I come face-to-face with my own mortality—which can be a little frightening.

As these women approached Christ's tomb, they had to be feeling a little fear and uncertainty. They were coming face-to-face with Christ's mortality. They knew why they were there: Jesus had been in the tomb since Friday night, and his body would have been starting to smell; so they had come to anoint Christ's body with spices. Jesus had been their teacher, their healer, their friend, and their Messiah; but now he was dead. They had seen him raise others from the dead—so as these women approached the tomb, they had to be wondering why Jesus hadn't done more to save himself.

Upon arriving at the tomb, these women found themselves in a very interesting—and unexpected—situation. While they were outside the tomb, a violent earthquake started when an angel of the Lord came down to roll back the stone that was covering the mouth of the cave. According to Matthew's account, the angel's appearance was like lightning and his clothes were as white as snow.

The scene was so overwhelming that even the experienced soldiers who had been guarding the tomb were so afraid that "they shook and became like dead men" (Matthew 28:4).

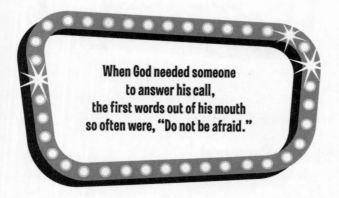

> **When God needed someone to answer his call, the first words out of his mouth so often were, "Do not be afraid."**

Not wanting the women to be paralyzed by fear, the angel said to the women, "Do not be afraid" (v. 5).

"Do not be afraid." What do those words mean to you?

Every person is afraid at one time or another. God knows us, and he knows that we have fear, so—throughout the Bible—when God needed someone to answer his call, the first words out of his mouth so often were, "Do not be afraid."

When Abram started to doubt that he would ever have a son, God said, "Do not be afraid" (Genesis 15:1).

When Moses and the Israelites found themselves facing King Og of Bashan and his army, God said, "Do not be afraid" (Numbers 21:34).

When Joshua was preparing to battle the city of Ai (after previously being defeated by them), God said, "Do not be afraid" (Joshua 8:1).

Game Show Trivia

In 1965, Christian recording artist Keith Green appeared on *I've Got a Secret* when he was only eleven years old. His secret was, "I just signed a five-year contract as a rock 'n' roll singer."[3]

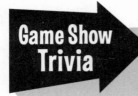

When the Israelites were facing the king of Babylon and his army, God said, "Do not be afraid" (Jeremiah 42:11).

When Mary was told that she was going to be the mother of the Messiah, the angel of the Lord said, "Do not be afraid" (Luke 1:30).

When Joseph found out that his virgin wife was going to have a baby, God said (through an angel), "Do not be afraid" (Matthew 1:20).

When Jesus was trying to prepare his disciples for the last day of his life, he said, "Do not be afraid" (John 14:27).

When Paul was being persecuted for preaching the gospel, God—wanting him to keep going and telling—said, "Do not be afraid" (Acts 18:9).

It's not a sin to be afraid; it's human. But it is a sin to allow fear to paralyze us and keep us from sharing the good news that Jesus is alive.

Jesus wanted these women to be bold as they shared their secret; so when he appeared to them as they left the tomb, he also said, "Do not be afraid" (Matthew 28:10).

Their secret was too important to be entombed by fear.

Our secret is too important too. We can't let fear win. As we tell the good news, it's OK to share the secret that we had to face our fears to do so, because that reveals that we are faithful, not fearful.

"Doubts Can Be Dealt With."

The angel knew that this secret about Jesus was unbelievable, so he told the women, "Come and see the place where he lay" (Matthew 28:6). He knew that if they saw with their own eyes that Jesus' body was gone, they'd be more apt to believe.

Doubt is not a sin. Like fear, it's just a part of being human. Our perspective is finite. We can't know everything, so there will be some things that never

Game Show Trivia

The cast of *I've Got a Secret* appeared on the cover of *TV Guide* magazine four times.

make sense. But like fear, our doubts—if left unchecked—can lead us to sin by hindering our faith.

Some of the most faithful people in the Bible had to deal with doubt.

Moses doubted his ability to communicate God's plan to Pharaoh and the Egyptians, so he asked God, "What if they do not believe me or listen to me and say, 'The Lord did not appear to you'?" (Exodus 4:1). But he didn't let those doubts stop him from telling Pharaoh to let the Israelites go.

Gideon doubted God's ability to defeat the Midianites: "'But Lord,' Gideon asked, 'how can I save Israel?'" (Judges 6:15). But he didn't let those doubts stop him from leading three hundred men to a decisive victory.

Peter doubted his own ability to keep walking on the water and cried out, "Lord, save me!" (Matthew 14:30). But he didn't let those doubts stop him from being the first person to step out with the gospel on the Day of Pentecost.

Thomas doubted when he heard of Christ's resurrection from the dead. He said, "Unless I see the nail marks in his hands and put my finger where the nails were, and put my hands into his side, I will not believe it" (John 20:25). But he didn't let those doubts stop him from touching his Savior and touching this world.

All believers will, at one time or another, have doubts. So with Jude I say, "Be merciful to those who doubt" (Jude 1:22). But all believers also have a responsibility to share God's good secrets with the world, so with Jesus I also say, "Stop doubting and believe" (John 20:27).

"Good Secrets Are Meant to Be Shared."

I'm so glad he didn't take his secret to the grave, because his secret has blessed my life, satisfied a hunger deep in my soul for something more, and helped me to grow in numerous ways.

Of course I'm talking about . . . Colonel Sanders—and his fried chicken with its secret blend of eleven herbs and spices.

Colonel Sanders knew that his secret recipe was the key to the success of his company, so he went to great lengths to protect it. As a result, only a handful of people know the multimillion dollar recipe. In addition, production is compartmentalized so that one company produces part of the spice blend and another company handles the other, with neither company having the complete recipe.

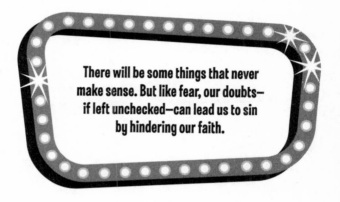

There will be some things that never make sense. But like fear, our doubts—if left unchecked—can lead us to sin by hindering our faith.

The Colonel once said, "It boggles the mind just to think of all the procedures and precautions the company takes to protect my recipe, especially when I think how Claudia and I used to operate. She was my packing girl, my warehouse supervisor, my delivery person—you name it. Our garage was the warehouse."[4]

But imagine if the Colonel had taken his secret to his grave. I am so grateful that he shared his secret with his team before it was too late!

God didn't want these women at the tomb to wait one more moment before telling their good news. Through the angel the Lord said, "Go quickly and tell his disciples: 'He has risen from the dead and is going ahead of you into Galilee. There you will see him'" (Matthew 28:7). The women didn't need to hear anything else and immediately hurried from the tomb with this good news.

I'm so glad they didn't procrastinate. But why would they? They had just heard the best news of all time! With the revelation of this secret, their prayers had been answered, their grief had been executed, their pain healed, their hearts mended, and their hope restored. Good secrets like that can't be untold.

Why do we procrastinate when it comes to sharing the good news that Jesus has risen from the dead? It's inexcusable. Too many Christians are taking this amazing secret to their graves when, if only they would tell it, the lives of countless people could be changed forever.

I'm so glad these women didn't take this secret to their graves, because this secret has blessed my life, satisfied a hunger deep in my soul for something more, and helped me to grow in numerous ways.

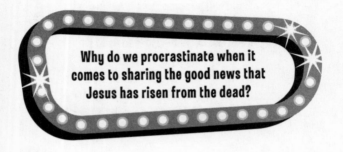

Why do we procrastinate when it comes to sharing the good news that Jesus has risen from the dead?

That's the thing about good secrets that aren't meant to be kept—they mean nothing unless they are shared. Some secrets have the power to give life, not take it. These secrets must not be kept; they must be shared.

Like this one: Jesus is alive! He's not here; he has risen.

Can you keep this secret?

I hope not.

Truth or Consequences

For individual or group study

For Personal Study and Reflection

Write down a symbol to represent a secret you know that—if revealed—could cause some bad things to happen. Next to the symbol, write down a few of the bad things that might happen if that secret were revealed. Now write down a symbol to represent a secret you know that—if revealed—could cause some good things to happen. What good things could happen if that secret were revealed?

For Group Study and Discussion

(Items needed: paper and pens) Play a game of I've Got a Secret with your group. As your group members arrive, ask each one to write down on a piece of paper a secret they don't mind revealing. They can keep the papers in their pockets. Select three or four members of your group to be on the panel. (The members of the panel don't need to write down a secret.) Play the game by selecting one member (or a couple if they share a secret) to be on the hot seat. One person needs to be the host. The host reads the secret (to himself) and then passes it to the people who are not on the panel. The host then gives the panel the category (i.e., "This secret has to do with something the person did" or "This secret has to do with somewhere the person went.") Each person on the panel gets twenty seconds to ask "yes" or "no" questions and then try to guess the secret. The round is over when someone properly guesses the secret.

Truth

Read Matthew 28:1-10.

1. God hasn't kept a lot of secrets from us. Sure, he hasn't told us when Christ is coming back again, but—besides that one—he has revealed everything we needed to know at the time we needed to know it.
Think about some of the secrets God has revealed in the Bible. Which one has had the biggest impact on your life? Why?

2. It's not a sin to be afraid; it's human. But it is a sin to allow fear to paralyze us and keep us from sharing the good news that Jesus is alive.
Share or reflect on a time when you had to face your fears to tell someone about Jesus. What did you learn from that experience?

3. That's the thing about good secrets that aren't meant to be kept—they mean nothing unless they are shared.
What is one of the best secrets that you've ever been told? What made it so great? What impact did that secret have on your life or the life of someone you know? Were you ever told a secret that you couldn't share with anybody at all? How did not being able to share it make you feel?

Consequences

Share or reflect on one thing you learned in this chapter about:

- yourself

- God

How will you use the lessons from this chapter to bring about positive consequences in the lives of the people in your world? Be specific.

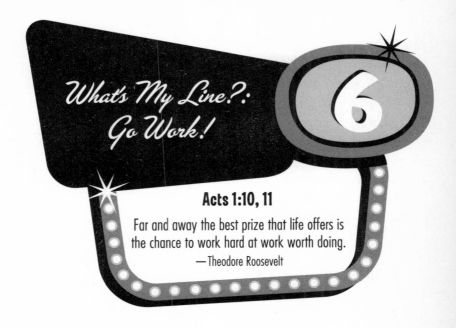

6

What's My Line?: Go Work!

Acts 1:10, 11

Far and away the best prize that life offers is the chance to work hard at work worth doing.
—Theodore Roosevelt

"What are your intentions?"

The journey of *Apollo 13* has been called a successful failure. NASA's *Apollo 13* mission was supposed to go to the moon, but a wiring malfunction caused the ship to lose power deep in space, leaving Commander Jim Lovell, Fred Haise, and Jack Swigert in a desperate fight for survival. Their job was no longer to explore the moon. Their job now was to get home alive and—as Gene Kranz said in his now famous quote—"Failure is not an option."

In his book *Apollo 13*, Jim Lovell recalls a significant exchange between himself and his crew at a crucial time in their mission.[1]

As the capsule emerged from the extremely tense twenty-minute journey around the dark side of the moon (during which the crew was out of radio contact with Mission Control in Houston), Lovell moved away from the capsule window so that Haise and Swigert could see the moon and take some pictures. Lovell had been to the moon before, but the other two had not. Lovell recalls that his crew stared at the moon in respectful silence—transfixed by the scene 139 miles below them. Five minutes passed as Haise and Swigert sat staring out the window, but Lovell had already gone back to preparing the capsule for an important procedure. Lovell recalls that he tried to maneuver around his crew, saying, "Excuse me, Freddo" and "I'm sorry, Jack," but they would only respond to him with a nod—absently moving out of his way for a moment before floating back to look out the window.

Eventually Lovell—having had enough of his crew staring out the window—asked an important question, "Gentlemen, what are your intentions?"

Startled, Haise and Swigert spun around.

"Our intentions?" Swigert said.

"Yes," said Lovell. "We have a PC+2 maneuver coming up. Is it your intention to participate in it?"

"Jim," Haise said somewhat feebly, "this is our last chance to get these shots. We've come all the way out here—don't you think they're going to want us to bring back some pictures?"

"If we don't get home, you'll never get those pictures developed," Lovell said.

With important work to be done, Jim Lovell didn't want his men to waste too much time staring out the window. He knew what his line was, and he wanted his men to know what their line was too. He expected them to get to work doing their jobs so they could all make it safely home.

What's Our Line?

You and I have important work to do too. But like Haise and Swigert, we are all too often distracted by the world that is quickly passing by just outside our window.

Game Show Trivia

The *What's My Line?* show consisted of four panelists trying to guess the unusual occupation of a guest. It was network television's longest-running primetime game show, with a broadcast run of over seventeen-and-one-half years.

This world—and the trials we face here—can too easily distract us from the work that God expects us to complete before he returns.

My dad was a loving father and a strong disciplinarian. When he told me to do something, he expected me to obey. If he told me to have the yard mowed before he arrived home from work at 5:30 PM, I knew that I had better do it.

But what if I didn't?

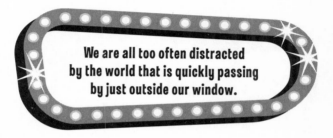

We are all too often distracted by the world that is quickly passing by just outside our window.

What if—instead of doing the work he asked me to do—I sat at the end of our driveway under an umbrella, in a lawn chair, with an ice-cold Coca-Cola, a guitar, one of my dad's old high school yearbooks, and wearing a T-shirt that read "In Dad I Trust"?

What if—instead of doing the work he asked me to do—I spent some of my time playing my guitar and singing songs that I'd written about my dad? Lyrics like "My dad is an awesome dad, he works at a college downtown" or "I could sing of Dad's love forever." Or my all-time favorite, "'Tis so sweet to trust my daddy, just to take him at his word."

What if—instead of doing the work he asked me to do—I spent some of my time looking at my dad's old yearbook, reading about all of his past exploits?

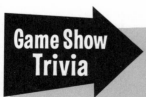

Game Show Trivia

Steve Allen was a regular panelist from 1953 to 1954 and was credited with asking what became one of the show's most famous questions: "Is it bigger than a bread box?"

What if—instead of doing the work he asked me to do—I spent some of my time walking around the block so that everyone in my neighborhood could see my T-shirt and know how much I loved my dad?

What if—instead of doing the work he asked me to do—I spent the whole day waiting for my dad to return home?

I don't really have to play the What If? game. I know that if I had chosen to disobey my dad, I would have been punished.

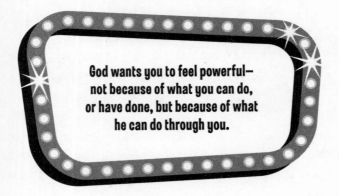

God wants you to feel powerful—not because of what you can do, or have done, but because of what he can do through you.

God loves to hear us sing about his love for us and our love for him. He loves for us to read the Book that tells about all he's done for us. He loves for us to let other people know how much we love him. But if we really want to show God how much we love him, then we'll get to work letting people know how much *he* loves *them.*

We Christians shouldn't have to ask, "What's my line?"

God was clear about what our line is when he said, "Go and make disciples of all nations, baptizing them in the name of the Father and of the Son and of the Holy Spirit, and teaching them to obey everything I have commanded you" (Matthew 28:19, 20).

Our job is to go! And as we go, we are to make disciples of all nations, baptizing them, and teaching them to obey. This is our line . . . our work . . . and failure is not an option.

There are a few things that are essential to completing our task.

Trust

Christ's disciples felt a little powerless, but Christ wanted them to feel powerful. Christ *needed* them to feel powerful, so he made them a promise: "You will receive power when the Holy Spirit comes on you" (Acts 1:8).

Not "You *might* receive power." Not "You can receive power." No, Jesus promised his disciples, "You *will* receive power" because he wanted them to trust him.

Trust in God's power is essential to the success of our work.

The word that is used here for *power* is the Greek word *dunamis*, from which we get our word *dynamite*. Do you feel like dynamite?

In his book *The Table of Inwardness*, Calvin Miller writes about a nineteenth-century wooden box that someone gave him many years ago.[2] He prized that box because of its meticulous craftsmanship. On it was written in large black and red letters: "Danger: Dynamite!" Miller writes, "At one time the box had indeed been dangerous; its contents had to be handled gently. But the last time I saw it, the box was filled with common paraphernalia that could be found in any workroom. . . . The box should have read, 'Danger: Junk—half bits of twine, a half-wound roll of tape, a crooked screwdriver.'"

Do you feel like a box of powerful dynamite or a box of powerless junk?

God wants you to feel powerful—not because of what you can do, or have done, but because of what he can do through you. With God in your life, the Holy Spirit in your soul (Acts 2:38), and your life safely hidden in Christ, you have all the power you're ever going to need to do all the things that God needs for you to do.

You have to trust this. God always gives us all the power we need for any job he calls us to do.

Game Show Trivia

On September 19, 1954, *What's My Line?* became the first panel show broadcast in color.

Game Show Trivia

The 876th and final network show aired on September 3, 1967.

The apostles had to trust this too. In Acts 2, when God's promise was realized and his power was poured out through the Holy Spirit, the Galilean disciples were given the power to speak in languages they didn't know (Acts 2:7, 8). Wow! What an amazing gift with such practical benefits. I think it would be awesome if God would give me the ability to speak Spanish. Then I could better communicate with people in my community today without bothering to go through the arduous process of having to learn Spanish on my own. In fact, I think it would be awesome for God to give me the ability to speak whatever language it is that the women in my house are speaking. Then I can better communicate with them today instead of bothering to go through the arduous process of having to learn their "language" on my own!

The ability to speak in other languages was going to be a crucial tool in the apostles' efforts to preach the gospel to people of all nations, but it wasn't the only tool they would be given. We know, from what we read in the rest of Acts, that the apostles also received the ability to perform miracles (Acts 3:6, 7).

God poured out his power because he wanted people to trust in him. But for that to happen, he needed people to trust the apostles. But for *that* to happen, he needed the apostles to trust in him.

God wants *us* to trust in him too. He has a big job for us to do, so he's given us plenty of power.

He's given us the power of the Bible.

"I am not ashamed of the gospel, because it is the power of God for the salvation of everyone who believes: first for the Jew, then for the Gentile" (Romans 1:16).

He's given us the power of the Holy Spirit.

"May the God of hope fill you with all joy and peace as you trust in him, so that you may overflow with hope by the power of the Holy Spirit" (Romans 15:13).

He's given us the power of salvation.

"The message of the cross is foolishness to those who are perishing, but to us who are being saved it is the power of God" (1 Corinthians 1:18).

He's given us the power of the kingdom of God.

"The kingdom of God is not a matter of talk but of power" (1 Corinthians 4:20).

He's given us the power that comes through assembling in the name of Jesus Christ.

"When you are assembled in the name of our Lord Jesus and I am with you in spirit, and the power of our Lord Jesus is present . . ." (1 Corinthians 5:4).

He's given us all the power we are ever going to need to do all we ask or imagine.

"Now to him who is able to do immeasurably more than all we ask or imagine, according to his power that is at work within us, to him be glory in the church and in Christ Jesus throughout all generations, for ever and ever! Amen" (Ephesians 3:20, 21).

As you work, ask for more, imagine more, and trust more.

Courage

The disciples were being asked to do a dangerous job.

After promising them power, the Lord also promised them problems: "And you will be my witnesses in Jerusalem, and in all Judea and Samaria, and to

Game Show Trivia

***What's My Line?* won the Emmy Award for the Best Quiz or Audience Participation Show three times—in 1952, 1953, and 1958.**

During a demonstration of tossing pizza, Gene Rayburn flipped one so high that it got stuck in the lights above the stage.

Game Show Trivia

the ends of the earth" (Acts 1:8). You may not see any problems in that verse. But when Jesus told them that they were going to be his "witnesses," he foretold the problems to come. The Greek word translated *witnesses* is the word *martus,* the root from which we get the word *martyr.*

With the word *witnesses,* the disciples heard what Jesus was really saying: he was telling them that they were going to have to be willing to do whatever it took to share their faith, even to the point of giving up their lives—which many of them did, in fact.

Would you pursue a job if it might cost you your life?

My wife and I are addicted to the TV show *The Deadliest Catch. The Deadliest Catch* chronicles the world of king crab fishermen in the Bering Sea. These men risk their lives, facing treacherous weather conditions, doing one of the deadliest jobs in the world.

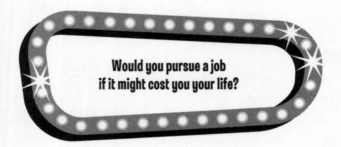

Would you pursue a job if it might cost you your life?

Throughout the years many men have died fishing for king crabs.[3]

In 1976, the ship *Master Carl* was returning home when it began to take on water. The four crew members abandoned ship and made it into a life raft, but only two were found alive.

In 1981, the ship *St. Patrick* tipped 90 degrees and took on water in the engine compartment. The eleven-man crew tied themselves together and leaped into the sea when the lifeboat was lost. Only two men survived.

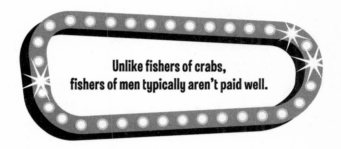

**Unlike fishers of crabs,
fishers of men typically aren't paid well.**

In 2002, the ship *Galaxy* caught fire at sea. All twenty-three crew members were rescued by the coast guard; three men later died from injuries received during the fire.

In 2005, during the first season of *The Deadliest Catch,* a boat named *Big Valley* sank. Five of the six crew members perished; three were never found.

It takes an unbelievable amount of courage to fish for king crabs on the Bering Sea. These fishermen are clearly risking their lives, but—after watching this show many times—I'm confident that these men aren't risking their lives for the love of catching crabs; they are risking their lives for a lot of money. King crab fishermen can earn $50,000 in three months of fishing on the Bering Sea.[4]

Unlike fishers of crabs, fishers of men typically aren't paid well. In fact, many fishers of men end up *paying* a high cost. Some of the best fishers of men paid with their lives: Stephen, Peter, Polycarp[5] . . . Chet Bitterman.

In 1981, while working as a linguist for Wycliffe Bible Translators, Chet Bitterman was captured by Colombian terrorists.[6] In the early morning hours of January 19, 1981, armed terrorists burst into the home where Bitterman and his family were staying in Bogotá. Bitterman was kidnapped. During his imprisonment, the terrorists demanded that all Wycliffe translators leave

Colombia or he would be killed. Forty-eight days into the ordeal, Bitterman was executed.

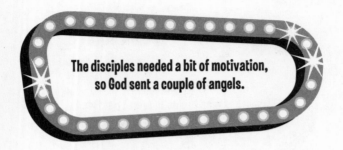

The disciples needed a bit of motivation, so God sent a couple of angels.

Chet Bitterman knew what his line was and had the courage to complete the task. This is evident in something Chet wrote in his journal two years before his execution at the hand of terrorists: "The situation in Nicaragua is getting worse. If Nicaragua falls, I guess the rest of Central America will too. Maybe this is just some kind of self-inflicted Martyr complex, but I find this reoccurring thought that perhaps God will call me to be martyred in His service in Colombia. I am willing."[7] His courage is also evident in a prayer he prayed shortly before his death: "Lord, the tribe that's the most remote, the most difficult to reach because of location and culture, the tribe no one else might select because of those reasons, Lord, if it's okay with you, that's my tribe."[8]

A year after Chet's murder, applications doubled for overseas work with Wycliffe. In the months and years that followed, several of the terrorists came to believe in Christ as a result of Bitterman's witness.[9]

Chet completed his task because he knew what his line was and because he had the courage needed to see the job through to the end.

Motivation

People are motivated by different things—money, fear, opportunity . . . and even angels.

Have you ever been motivated by angels? The disciples were.

Jesus had been crystal clear about what he wanted them to do: "You will be my witnesses in Jerusalem, and in all Judea and Samaria, and to the ends of the earth" (Acts 1:8). Jesus their Lord wanted them to take the gospel to their city, then to their country, and then to the rest of the world—and then he was taken up into a cloud right before their eyes. After a clear command followed by an amazing departure, the disciples did what many of us would have done after seeing such an obviously divine event—they just stood there . . . looking intently "up into the sky" (Acts 1:10).

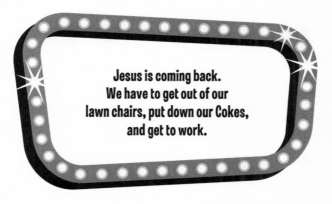

**Jesus is coming back.
We have to get out of our
lawn chairs, put down our Cokes,
and get to work.**

The disciples needed a bit of motivation, so God sent a couple of angels.

"Men of Galilee," they said, "what are your intentions?"

Well, that's not exactly what the angels asked, but it's what they meant when they asked, "Why do you stand here looking into the sky? This same Jesus, who has been taken from you into heaven, will come back in the same way you have seen him go into heaven" (Acts 1:11).

Jesus is coming back. We have to get out of our lawn chairs, put down our Cokes, and get to work because there's still so much to do. Speaking of Coca-Cola . . . did you know:

- 97 percent of the world has heard of Coca-Cola?[10]
- 72 percent of the world has seen a can of Coca-Cola?

- 51 percent of the world has tasted a can of Coca-Cola?
- Coca-Cola has been around for only 104 years?

If God had given the job of world evangelization to The Coca-Cola Company, it would most likely be done by now.[11]

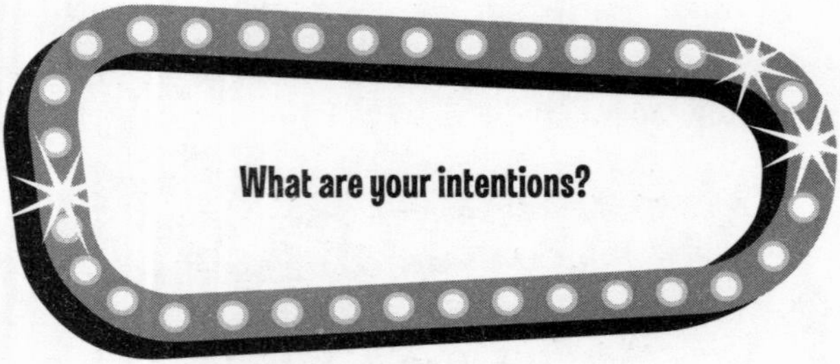
What are your intentions?

Are we as motivated to share the gospel? Speaking of motivation . . . did you know:

- there are 865 million unreached Muslims or Islamic followers in 3,330 cultural subgroupings?[12]
- there are 550 million unreached Hindus?
- there are 150 million unreached Chinese?
- there are 275 million unreached Buddhists?
- there are 2,550 unreached tribal groups (which are mainly animistic), with a total population of 140 million?
- there are 17 million unreached Jews scattered across 134 countries?

There you go. Will you go? What are your intentions?

Our job is to go! And as we go, we are to make disciples of all nations, baptizing them, and teaching them to obey.

This is our line . . . our work.

And failure is not an option.

Truth or Consequences

For individual or group study

For Personal Study and Reflection

List all the jobs you've had. Put a slash through the job that was the worst. Next to that job, write one sentence explaining why it was your worst job. Now circle the job that was your favorite. Next to that job, write a sentence explaining why it was your favorite.

For Group Study and Discussion

Begin your group time by asking members to name the worst jobs they've ever had and to tell why they were the worst. Now take turns sharing the best jobs you've ever had, also explaining why.

Truth

Read Matthew 28:16-20 and Acts 1:1-11.

1. *This world—and the trials we face here—can too easily distract us from the work that God expects us to complete before he returns.*
What are some of the most common trials faced by the people you know? In what ways can those trials be a distraction from the work that God expects us to do?

2. Do you feel like a box of powerful dynamite or a box of powerless junk?
Share or reflect on a time when you felt powerless. Why did you feel powerless? Now consider a time when you felt powerful. Why did you feel powerful? Do you feel powerful or powerless right now? Why?

3. God always gives us all the power we need for any job he calls us to do.
Share or reflect on a past job that you believe God called you to do. What was the job? How did God call you? How did God empower you for that job?

4. People are motivated by different things.
In your opinion, what is one of the biggest motivators for the people you know? Why? What is one of the biggest motivators in your life? Why? What does your motivator say about you? If you're not happy with what your motivator says about you, what is one thing you can do this week to make a positive change?

Consequences

Share or reflect on one thing you learned in this chapter about:

- yourself

- God

How will you use the lessons from this chapter to bring about positive consequences in the lives of the people in your world? Be specific.

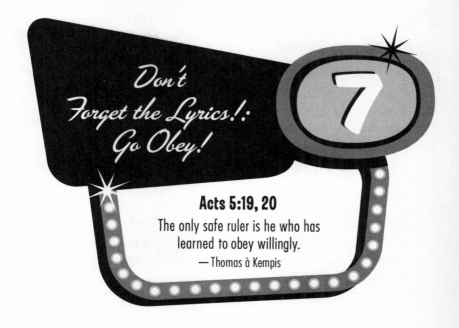

7 Don't Forget the Lyrics!: Go Obey!

Acts 5:19, 20

The only safe ruler is he who has learned to obey willingly.

—Thomas à Kempis

Caroline Marcil became famous for all the wrong reasons.

She was given a wonderful opportunity to display her musical talent by singing the national anthems of both Canada and the United States before an exhibition hockey game between the Canadian and United States national teams on April 22, 2005.[1] However, partway through "The Star Spangled Banner" she forgot the words—twice! After apologizing to the crowd, Marcil left the ice and headed back toward the dressing room—presumably to get the words. When she left the ice, many of the 7,166 fans in the Quebec Coliseum started to boo.

For a singer, there's nothing much worse than forgetting the lyrics.

When Marcil came back with lyrics in hand to finish the song, things got worse. As Marcil returned to the ice, the carpet she was supposed to stand on slipped out from underneath her, causing her to fall backwards onto the ice. After lying motionless on the ice for a few seconds, she got up and left the rink on her own—unhurt, but embarrassed that more than seven thousand people saw her forget the lyrics *and* fall on the ice.

Game Show Trivia

Wayne Brady (host of *Don't Forget the Lyrics!*) and Joey Fatone (host of the competing show *The Singing Bee*) both attended Dr. Phillips High School in Orlando, Florida.

She didn't realize that things could actually get worse than that, but they did.

That evening, and the rest of the weekend, Marcil's embarrassing moment was played endlessly on TV stations across North America, including on Fox News, CNN, and *The Tonight Show* with Jay Leno.[2] Millions of people saw Marcil's lapse of memory and footing.

Two days later Marcil sang the song on the Sunday morning broadcast of the ABC morning news show *Good Morning America* without a problem.

That makes me happy.

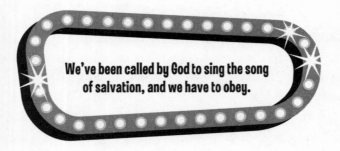

We've been called by God to sing the song of salvation, and we have to obey.

I'm so glad she didn't give up.

The fact that Marcil got up off that ice, pulled herself together, and refused to let the lyrics to "The Star Spangled Banner" go unsung says a lot about her character. Sure, she didn't sing all the lyrics that night she fell on the ice—because she had been traumatized by the events of that evening and couldn't bear to go out in front of those people again. But she refused to hide. She refused to let the lyrics to the national anthem of the United States go unsung.

On the Monday after her "moment" on the ice, she was on ABC again, explaining why she needed to return to the ice. In accented English she said, "I wanted to do it and to show I was able to do it. I go get my words and—I'm going to do this song. I have to."[3]

Singing the Song

We have to.

We are the singers. We've been called by God to sing the song of salvation, and we have to obey. The gospel is our song. We have to sing it until the world knows it so well that they can sing it with us. Not singing the lyrics—not finishing the song that Christ started—is not an option.

We may fail—or fall—but like Caroline Marcil, we must get up, pull ourselves together, and refuse to let the lyrics of the gospel go unsung.

Satan wants us to forget the lyrics. He wants to beat the tune out of our hearts until even the memory of the melody is forgotten. He hates the song. The song torments him, reminding him that he is doomed; so he prowls around seeking to devour all singers of the song. The silenced song is his dream, and causing singers to forget the lyrics is the first step toward making his dream a reality.

Satan wanted the apostles to forget the lyrics. He must have been pleased when the Sadducees arrested the apostles and put them in a public jail. The apostles had been singing the song in Solomon's Colonnade (Acts 5:12), and many people were changing their tune because of its tune. People were being healed, evil spirits were being cast out . . . and the Sadducees were upset.

The Sadducees were members of a Jewish political party that denied the resurrection of the body, the existence of angels and spirits, and were—based on what we see in the New Testament—more concerned with worldly things than with spiritual. In Acts, Luke explained that they were jealous of the apostles and the attention they were getting. They were annoyed by the song. They wanted it silenced, so they arrested the apostles and had them put in a public jail.

During the night an angel of the Lord opened the doors to their cell, brought them out, and said, "Go, stand in the temple courts . . . and tell the people the full message of new life" (Acts 5:19, 20).

Obedience

God expects obedience and faithfulness from his singers. He expects us to go when he says to go. Each of the men and women we have studied in this book had a choice when God told them, "Go!" They could choose to obey or not. They could have decided to disobey and stay, but—thankfully—they decided to obey and go. Going is an option, but for the true follower of Jesus, going is not optional. A follower of Christ follows Christ. It sounds like a riddle, but we can't be followers of Christ if we won't follow Christ. God had a plan, and God's plans can't be thwarted (Acts 5:39). He commanded the apostles to go to the temple courts and sing the song of salvation, and that's exactly what they did.

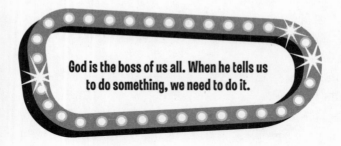

God is the boss of us all. When he tells us to do something, we need to do it.

"At daybreak they entered the temple courts, as they had been told, and began to teach the people" (Acts 5:21).

Do we do as we're told?

Last night my younger daughter, Payton, came into the living room to tell on her brothers: "They are telling me that I have to leave their room, but they're not the boss of me!" she exclaimed.

Right. You're not the boss of me, and I'm not the boss of you. I'm not even the boss of *me,* and you're not the boss of you either.

Game Show Trivia

In its debut, *Don't Forget the Lyrics!* averaged 3.4 million viewers among adults ages eighteen to forty-nine.

God is the boss of us all. When he tells us to do something, we need to do it.

The apostles understood this. After being discovered preaching in the temple courts again, the apostles were brought before the Sanhedrin to be questioned by the high priest. Peter and the other apostles responded, "We must obey God rather than men!" (v. 29).

And we must too.

Our society says, "If it feels good do it." But God says, "Be holy" (Leviticus 11:44; Hebrews 12:14; 1 Peter 1:16).

Psychologists say, "Learning to love yourself is the greatest love of all." But God says, "'Love the Lord your God with all your heart and with all your soul and with all your mind.' This is the first and greatest commandment. And the second is like it: 'Love your neighbor as yourself'" (Matthew 22:37-39).

Today's culture says, "He who dies with the most toys wins." But God says, "Do not store up for yourselves treasures on earth, where moth and rust destroy, and where thieves break in and steal. But store up for yourselves treasures in heaven, where moth and rust do not destroy, and where thieves do not break in and steal" (Matthew 6:19, 20).

We say, "You're not the boss of me!" But God says, "You must obey my laws and be careful to follow my decrees. I am the LORD your God" (Leviticus 18:4).

Men say, "We gave you strict orders not to teach in this name" (Acts 5:28), but godly men say, "We must obey God rather than men!" (Acts 5:29).

And we must too, but we must do so faithfully.

Faithfulness

There's no such thing as being partially faithful. You either are or you aren't.

Abraham either left Haran or he didn't.

Gideon either faced the Midianites or he didn't.

Hannah either gave Samuel to God or she didn't.

Esther either confronted Xerxes or she didn't.

The women either told the good news of Christ's resurrection or they didn't.

The disciples either stopped looking intently into the sky and got busy or they didn't.

And the apostles either told people the full message of God or they didn't.

Singing only part of the gospel lyrics wasn't an option. They were to be obedient in singing all the lyrics—the full message. If they had "forgotten" some of the lyrics, merely humming the words of the song of salvation . . . well, that wasn't going to be enough to save a lost and dying world. And it would have rendered the apostles disobedient and unfaithful.

Faithfulness requires that we sing all the lyrics, that we preach the full message of God.

Some children were asked, "What is love?" One little girl answered, "Love is when your mommy reads you a bedtime story. True love is when she doesn't skip any pages."[4]

If we truly love God and the people in this world, we won't skip—or forget—any lyrics as we sing them the song of salvation.

The apostles sang the song every chance they had, and they faithfully sang every word.

What did they sing? What are the lyrics we must not forget? We see them in the song the apostles sang before the Sanhedrin.

"God Raised Jesus"

The Sanhedrin was the Supreme Court of ancient Israel. As Peter and the other apostles stood before this council, they preached the full message of God, saying, "The God of our fathers raised Jesus from the dead—whom you had killed by hanging him on a tree" (Acts 5:30).

The apostles were putting themselves at great risk in this act of obedience. They were labeling as killers this group of people who crucified Jesus. These apostles were risking their very lives by not leaving out any lyrics.

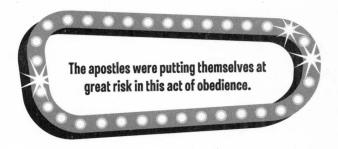

The apostles were putting themselves at great risk in this act of obedience.

What would you have done in this situation? Facing such a dangerous scenario, would you have forgotten the lyrics?

Would you have said, "I'm really sorry. This is a little awkward, but I need to tell you something. Um . . . is it hot in here? I'm kind of . . . anyway . . . um, what I need to tell you—and I don't want to hurt your feelings—but . . . you kind of messed up. Oh, I know you didn't mean to . . . and I'm sure it was an honest mistake . . . but you accidentally killed Jesus"?

I hope that's not the song you would have sung. These men didn't accidentally kill Jesus; they intentionally had him killed.

That's the truth, the whole truth, and nothing but the truth. And that's what this world needs to hear. They need to hear the whole truth—and the whole truth is that Jesus died on a cross but God raised him back to life again.

Game Show Trivia

In September 2007 when Gabrielle Hatchet saw the song titles "I Finally Got the Ring" and "Will You Marry Me?" she didn't realize at first that it was a setup by her boyfriend, Nathan Reid, to propose to her. Once she caught on, she promptly accepted and went on to win $350,000.

A man walking down the street saw in a store window a very beautiful picture of the crucifixion. As he gazed spellbound at the vividly pictured story, he suddenly became conscious that at his side stood a young boy. The boy too was gazing at the picture, and his tense expression made the man know that *The Crucifixion* had really gripped the eager little soul. Touching the boy on the shoulder, the man said, "Sonny, what does it mean?"

"Don't cha know?" the boy answered, his face full of marvel at the man's ignorance. "That there man is Jesus, an' them others is Roman soldiers, an' the woman what's cryin' is his mother, an' . . . they killed 'im!"

The man did not want to move from in front of that impressive piece of artwork, but he had other things to do. He turned and walked away. In a few moments he heard footsteps on the street behind him, and there came the boy rushing to catch him.

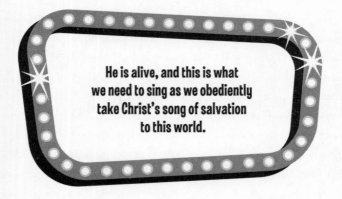

He is alive, and this is what we need to sing as we obediently take Christ's song of salvation to this world.

"Say, mister," he exclaimed breathlessly, "I forgot to tell you, but he rose again!"

We must not forget. We must run to tell people that Jesus rose again, because his resurrection makes everything matter. If Jesus is still in the tomb, our church buildings should be burned to the ground, every Christian bookstore should be closed, all missionaries need to be brought home and their slides of hungry children thrown into the nearest dumpster, all evangelistic broadcasts should be pulled off the airwaves, all Bibles should be shredded and the paper be used to line birdcages, you should immediately stop reading this book, and one of us needs to find Marilyn Manson and apologize to him. As Paul says, "If Christ has not been raised, our preaching is useless and so is your faith" (1 Corinthians 15:14).

Other religious leaders have died and been buried.

Siddhartha Gautama, who probably lived from 563–483 BC, was born into a wealthy Hindu family.[5] Sickened by the suffering he saw around him, he left his wife and son and searched for enlightenment. After six years, having been reduced to skin and bones, he sat down under a tree near the river Gaya. During meditation he received "enlightenment" and became "Buddha." Today, millions of people call themselves Buddhists. But Siddhartha Gautama is not alive. His ashes were divided into eight portions and buried under mounds raised in his hometown and at seven other locations.

Muhammad was born in AD 570 in the town of Mecca.[6] At age forty he claimed to receive revelations, which he wrote down as the Koran. He became a military leader, killing those who opposed Islam and leading ten thousand men to conquer Mecca and impose Islam on the people. In AD 632, Muhammad returned to Mecca one last time to perform a pilgrimage, and tens of thousands of Muslims joined him. Three months later he died there after a brief illness. He is buried in the mosque in Medina. Muhammad is not alive.

So don't call Marilyn Manson just yet, because—unlike these other religious leaders—Jesus is not in the tomb or buried anywhere. He is alive, and this is what we need to sing as we obediently take Christ's song of salvation to this world.

But these aren't all the lyrics; there are more.

Game Show Trivia

San Francisco 49ers legend Jerry Rice made an appearance on *Don't Forget the Lyrics!* to help out contestant Michael Oliver after Michael got off to a shaky start.

"So You Could Be Raised Too"

As the apostles continued with the full message about Jesus, they told the Sanhedrin, "God exalted him to his own right hand as Prince and Savior that he might give repentance and forgiveness of sins to Israel" (Acts 5:31).

This was good news, but it was not received as such. This message struck a wrong chord with these Jewish leaders. They didn't want to hear that they had sinned, they didn't want to hear that their only hope for repentance and forgiveness was in the person of the "blasphemer" they had nailed to a cross, and they definitely didn't want to hear this news from these ragtag radical convicts.

These religious leaders were feeling buried by guilt. At one point in this event, they said to the apostles, "You have filled Jerusalem with your teaching and are determined to make us guilty of [Jesus'] blood" (Acts 5:28). But that wasn't the apostles' ultimate goal. The apostles weren't trying to bury these men; they were trying to raise these men. They wanted to raise their hopes—and their souls—by letting them know that the man they had killed died to save them.

These lyrics were some of the most important of all.

Guilt without hope brings misery.

An incomplete song by the apostles would have left all of Israel—and the rest of us—without hope. All the lyrics had to be sung: "God raised Jesus so you could be raised too." It's the same tune Paul sang when he reminded the Corinthian Christians: "Christ has indeed been raised from the dead, the firstfruits of those who have fallen asleep. For since death came through a man, the resurrection of the dead comes also through a man. For as in Adam all die, so in Christ all will be made alive" (1 Corinthians 15:20-22).

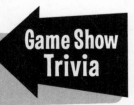

Game Show Trivia

Dottie Harris was the first contestant to make it to $500,000 before she passed on the Million Dollar Song opportunity. The song was not revealed.

We Have to Sing Along

Long ago I read the story of a father who passed a cemetery every day as he drove his two preschoolers to their day care. And at that spot each day, his son Tim would remind his younger sister, "Janna, that's where the dead people are." Janna was almost three years of age, and the idea of death was somewhat confusing to her. Her brother explained that the cemetery is where they bury people's bodies in the ground when they are dead, and their spirits go back to God. Several months later on Memorial Day, their family went for a bike ride. Janna rode behind her father in a bike trailer. With helmet on and her eyes darting from side to side, Janna, along with her family, enjoyed the fresh air and sunshine of that day.

Then they rode by the cemetery. It was filled with flowers and flags, and Janna saw people everywhere. Some huddled in groups; others knelt alone in front of headstones. From the bike trailer behind her father, Janna began to shout, "They're alive! They're alive! Daddy, they're alive!" It may have been Memorial Day, but for Janna it was Easter.

Every day is Easter for everyone who hears Christ's song of salvation and chooses to sing along. This truth kept the apostles singing for the rest of their lives.

The apostles were flogged and ordered not to speak in the name of Jesus ever again, but Luke records that they decided to obey God rather than men. After leaving the Sanhedrin, the apostles rejoiced because "they had been counted worthy of suffering disgrace for the Name" (Acts 5:41). We're told that "day after day, in the temple courts and from house to house, they never stopped teaching and proclaiming the good news that Jesus is the Christ" (Acts 5:42).

Game Show Trivia

The launch of *Don't Forget the Lyrics!* prompted NBC to move up the debut of their similar game show, *The Singing Bee.*

I'm glad they didn't give up. They were obedient. They didn't forget the lyrics. They kept singing with the hope that you and I would join the song and help others to join in too.

We must keep singing. Everyone in this world must have the chance to join the song.

Wouldn't it be amazing to hear the whole world singing the song of salvation?

It would be beautiful music to God's ears.

Truth or Consequences

For individual or group study

For Personal Study and Reflection

In the space below write the lyrics to your favorite song.

Reflect on why this is your favorite song. Circle the lyrics that mean the most to you right now.

For Group Study and Discussion

(Items needed: members' favorite CDs, CD player) Ahead of time, ask group members each to bring a CD that contains one of their favorite songs. Begin your group time by playing a portion of every member's favorite song. Encourage the group to sing along if they'd like to. Then work through the following questions:

- Do you remember when you first heard this song? What was the occasion?
- What memories does this song bring to mind?
- Which lyrics are your favorites? Why?

Truth

Read Acts 5:17-42.

1. *Satan wants us to forget the lyrics. He wants to beat the tune out of our hearts until even the memory of the melody is forgotten.*
Share or reflect on a time when you felt personally attacked by Satan. What was the nature of his attack (i.e., spiritual, financial, physical)? What things helped you most during that difficult time?

2. Guilt without hope brings misery.
Share or reflect on a time when you felt guilty as a child. Why did you feel guilty? How did the guilt affect your life at that time? Recall how you moved from feeling guilty to feeling hopeful in that situation. What gave you the hope that everything was going to be OK?

3. God is the boss of us all. When he tells us to do something, we need to do it.
Share or reflect on a time when you did something that you know God wanted you to do. Were you motivated more by fear or love? Why? What were some of the results of your obedience?

4. We must run to tell people that Jesus rose again, because his resurrection makes everything matter.
How has Christ's resurrection impacted the way you work? play? raise your kids? interact with your spouse? Now choose one of those realms and consider how that area of your life would be different if Christ were still in his tomb. How does that make you feel? How has Christ's resurrection made your life matter? Be specific.

Consequences

Share or reflect on one thing you learned in this chapter about:

- yourself

- God

How will you use the lessons from this chapter to bring about positive consequences in the lives of the people in your world? Be specific.

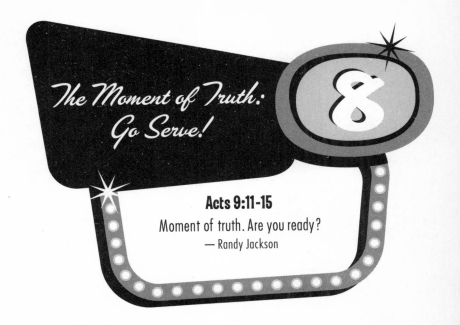

8

The Moment of Truth: Go Serve!

Acts 9:11-15

Moment of truth. Are you ready?
— Randy Jackson

Moment of truth. Are you ready?

Frank wasn't.

In one of the most controversial moments in television history, eight million viewers watched as the scales fell off Frank Cleri's eyes, and he saw his wife for who she really was. As the episode of *The Moment of Truth* began, host Mark L. Walberg provided a disclaimer—explaining to the audience watching at home that he opposed the airing of this particular episode due to the fact that it was too disturbing.[1]

That was an understatement.

Frank Cleri sat stunned as his wife Lauren confessed that she had been unfaithful to him and wished that she was married to her old boyfriend. Lauren later admitted that she went on the show in a bid for fame and fortune. In an article about this event in the *New York Post*, Lauren was quoted as saying, "If I'm going to end my marriage, then if I can win a hundred thousand or two hundred thousand dollars. I can start a new life with some cash in my pocket."[2]

But things didn't work out the way Lauren thought they would.

After admitting that she cheated on Frank (which netted her another $100,000), she was asked whether she considered herself a good person. She answered yes, but the lie-detector test said she was lying. She lost all the money . . . and probably her husband.

Frank had a choice to make. Ironically, because of Lauren's lies, *he* was now at a moment of truth. His life had changed in a single moment, and he had to decide what he was going to do next.

Moments of truth are great opportunities. Usually, a moment of truth provides you with a clear choice to make.

In the summer of 1988, I was in the middle of nowhere when I found myself at a moment of truth.

I had just finished my first year at Bible college, training to become a minister, when I headed to Yellowstone National Park for a summer job. Not sure what I wanted to do with my life, I thought Yellowstone would be a great place to figure some things out. And it was.

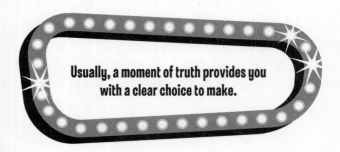

Usually, a moment of truth provides you with a clear choice to make.

While working at Yellowstone my faith was tested—not by God but by me. I spent a lot of time that summer trying to resolve whether or not the path I was following toward full-time Christian service was my choice or something else. The question I wanted to answer that summer was: Was I going into ministry because it was what I felt called to do or because it was what I was expected to do?

Game Show Trivia

***The Moment of Truth* is an American show that first aired in Colombia as *Nada más que la verdad* (*Nothing But the Truth*).**

So that summer, while waiting tables and working road construction, I spent a lot of time questioning my faith and my calling—that is, until I found myself at a moment of truth.

One cold, dark night in late summer, while working on a remote road in the middle of Yellowstone National Park, I received a message over the radio that I was supposed to report to the nearest ranger station. Whatever it was, I could tell it was important because I was quickly picked up in a truck and driven down the mountain where I was told to call home now. During that call I learned that my father had died the day before, and my family had been trying to reach me for about twelve hours.

Immediately, something like scales fell off my eyes.

Everything suddenly became crystal clear and—I know this may sound strange—in that moment of truth, I knew that I loved God more than anything and wanted to spend the rest of my life serving him.

I went back to school the next fall committed to serving God with every fiber of my being for every moment of my life, which is exactly what I've been doing since that dark night twenty years ago.

Serving Well

God has a plan for your life—and it's not to sit around and collect dust until you assume room temperature. God wants you and me to make a difference in this world by serving him. It's why he sent Jesus. In Revelation, John writes, "To him who loves us and has freed us from our sins by his blood, and has made us to be a kingdom and priests to *serve his God and Father*—to him be glory and power for ever and ever!" (Revelation 1:6, emphasis added). We were freed so that we could serve him well.

I've fallen in love with a restaurant across the street from my new church, called The Egg & I. I've eaten there a couple of times a week since I moved here two months ago. And it's not just because it's convenient and their pancakes are amazing; I keep going back because the service is so good. The servers call me by name, keep my water glass full, serve my eggs and bacon on a separate plate (just the way I like it), and treat me like royalty. They go out of their way to make me feel special. Just last week the owners of the restaurant mailed me two $10 gift certificates just to thank me for my business. Now that's what I call service.

God deserves good service too.

In the ninth chapter of Acts we find an event that revealed a few of the keys to giving God the kind of service he deserves.

Availability

God had a plan that involved a Jewish leader named Saul, who would serve him by going to the Gentiles, their kings, and the Jews. He would tell them that the guy who started the religion of the people that he'd been hunting down and persecuting—Jesus Christ—was now his Savior and desired to be their Savior too. But for this plan to work, God first needed an available disciple to become involved. He chose a man named Ananias. Ananias was living in Damascus when the Lord appeared to him in a vision and called him by name (Acts 9:10).

"Ananias!"

"Yes, Lord," he answered.

What's the first word that comes out of your mouth when God calls you? Do you say, "What?" or "Wait" or "No"?

Game Show Trivia

The first episode appeared right after the highly rated *American Idol* and managed to rate very well itself with 23 million viewers, the highest rating for a premiere to that point in 2008.

The first word out of Ananias's mouth was the word yes. That tells me a lot about Ananias and why God chose him to serve him in such a special way.

My friend Mark and I love gospel music. When we worked together at a church, we were known to turn on Kirk Franklin in the middle of a stressful afternoon and have a little "church" in the hallway between our offices! Invariably, in the middle of our singing—and exceptional dancing—a crowd would gather as Mark would yell out, "Arron, do you have a 'yes' in your spirit?"

"Yes, my brother, I have a 'yes' in my spirit!" I would reply, and then I asked him the same question. The answer Mark gave was always, "Yes! I've got a 'yes' in my spirit!"

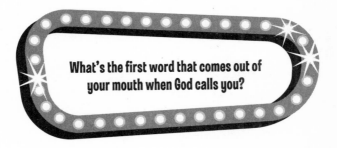

What's the first word that comes out of your mouth when God calls you?

Mark and I do have a "yes" in our spirits. We both know—from personal experience—that we are serving a God of possibilities.

We aren't serving a "no" God.

With God there's always a way, so there is no way I'm going to tell him no.

It may look like a dead end, but we serve a "yes" Lord!

It may look like it's terminal, but we serve a "yes" Lord!

It may look like certain divorce, but we serve a "yes" Lord!

Game Show Trivia

The show premiered on the Fox Channel January 23, 2008.

It may look like it's too broken to be fixed, but we serve a "yes" Lord!

It may look hopeless, but we serve a "yes" Lord. So when he calls us unexpectedly to do something that may seem impossible, we must say, "Yes."

Availability is the first key to giving God the kind of service he deserves. Ananias's reply tells me that he was available even before he knew what he was being called to do. He had a "yes" in his spirit.

The Lord told him, "Go to the house of Judas on Straight Street and ask for a man from Tarsus named Saul, for he is praying. In a vision he has seen a man named Ananias come and place his hands on him to restore his sight" (Acts 9:11, 12).

I love the fact that Ananias was already there! Without going anywhere, he was already with Saul—not physically but in a vision. God knew that he could count on Ananias to make himself available; he already saw Ananias going to Saul, so he made sure that Saul saw it too.

God knew that Ananias was available to serve.

Boldness

That doesn't mean that Ananias wasn't afraid.

"Lord," Ananias answered, "I have heard many reports about this man and all the harm he has done to your saints in Jerusalem. And he has come here with authority from the chief priests to arrest all who call on your name" (Acts 9:13, 14).

Ananias found himself at a moment of truth. Ananias knew that when Saul met him and learned that he was a follower of Christ, his freedom—and probably his life—would be in danger.

Saul was a bad man.

Saul was the man who oversaw the execution (stoning) of the apostle Stephen (Acts 7:57–8:1). He was obsessed with hunting down Christians, persecuting them, and taking them back as prisoners to Jerusalem (Acts 9:2), ripping them away from their homes, their spouses, and their children. Suffice it to say, Ananias had plenty of reasons to be afraid when God told him to go find Saul.

Imagine how you would feel if God told you to put on your "Proud to be an American!" T-shirt and go to a cave in Afghanistan for a get-to-know-you meeting with Osama bin Laden.

Now do you understand?

At first, Ananias couldn't see it. He didn't understand why the Lord was asking him to put himself in harm's way.

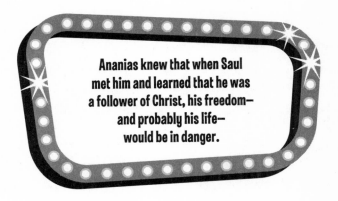

Ananias knew that when Saul met him and learned that he was a follower of Christ, his freedom—and probably his life—would be in danger.

A couple of months ago, my family and I moved to Colorado. This is such a great place to live. We've already been to the mountains a few times and have taken a few hikes. While on one hike with some new friends, they told us to make sure that we kept our little kids between us to prevent them from being taken by mountain lions.

What?!

Since we love living here and plan to continue doing a lot of hiking, I did some research on mountain lions to find out how to avoid or survive an encounter with a mountain lion on the trail.[3]

Don'ts:

- Don't hike, bike, or jog *alone* in lion territory.
- Don't try to sooth a lion verbally, as this may backfire.
- Don't act afraid of a lion you encounter.

- Don't bend over, crouch, or kneel.
- Never turn your back on a lion.
- Never, never run from a lion.

Do's:

- Keep children and pets in sight at all times.
- Always look up and behind you. Stay vigilant.
- If you do encounter a lion, try to give it a way out.
- Look a lion in the eye.
- Make loud, firm noises. You may even show your teeth and snarl.
- Use anything available as a weapon if the lion displays aggression. Carry pepper spray in easy reach. Use fists, sticks, rocks, tools, a pocketknife, a bicycle . . . whatever you can hit with, throw, and/or use as a shield.
- Make yourself look big. Open wide your coat, jacket, or any other item. Stand up straight, and swell your chest. Put small children on your shoulders to appear larger.

I love that last tip: make yourself look big. With God we don't have to act like we are bigger than we are, because with God we are big enough.

Ananias didn't need to make himself bigger; he just had to be bolder. So God gave him a little more encouragement, saying, "Go! This man is my chosen instrument to carry my name before the Gentiles and their kings and before the people of Israel. I will show him how much he must suffer for my name" (Acts 9:15, 16).

At this point something like scales fell from Ananias's eyes and—no longer afraid—he boldly went to serve God by serving Saul.

Contestants on *The Moment of Truth* answer twenty-one increasingly personal and embarrassing questions to receive cash prizes. They only receive a prize if a previously taken lie detector test indicates they are telling the truth. As of August 2008 no contestant had answered all questions truthfully according to the polygraph.

Game Show Trivia

Connection

The best service is all about connection.

Think about it. You will drive all the way across town to buy groceries from the store with the bag boy who knows that you prefer paper to plastic. You pay a little extra to get your dry cleaning done at the shop where they know—without asking—that you prefer light starch in your shirts. You will wait in a long line at the busiest Starbucks in town—even though the one closest to your office is not as busy—because the latte boy knows that you like your double latte with extra foam.

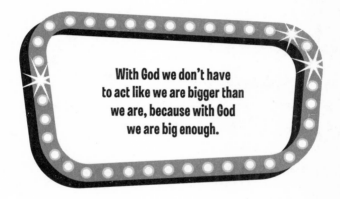

> **With God we don't have to act like we are bigger than we are, because with God we are big enough.**

When I trained servers at Olive Garden, I encouraged them to make connections with their guests by asking them about their kids, finding out what they were celebrating, looking them in the eye, asking their names, and a variety of things that would help them relate to their guests and show that they really cared.

God really cared about Saul, so he sent Ananias to take care of this man who had been sitting in darkness and not eating for three days (Acts 9:9). Because God really cared for Saul—and the countless people he would reach with the gospel—he wanted Ananias to "place his hands" (Acts 9:12) lovingly on a man who had placed his hands so severely on those who belonged to the Way (Acts 9:2). God wanted Ananias to connect with Saul, and that's what Ananias did.

Ananias placed his hands on Saul and said, "Brother Saul, the Lord—Jesus, who appeared to you on the road as you were coming here—has sent me so that you may see again and be filled with the Holy Spirit" (Acts 9:17).

Ananias (the Christ follower) called Saul (the persecutor of Christ followers) . . . brother. What an act of kindness! What an act of grace! What an act of love!

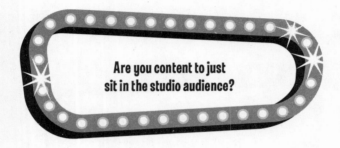

Are you content to just sit in the studio audience?

With this greeting, Ananias connected with Saul in a profound way.

In his book *Deliver Us From Evil*, Ravi Zacharias tells of Joseph Damien, a Belgian priest, who felt led to work among the lepers of Hawaii who were outcasts on the island of Molokai.[4] Surrounding their locations were huge cliffs so that one couldn't escape. The priest committed to work among them, to serve them, and to connect with them. Every morning for chapel he always began his message by saying, "My fellow believers." One day before chapel he spilled boiling water on his foot. To his horror, he realized he didn't feel the scalding. He knew then that he had leprosy. From then on he began his chapel messages by saying, "My fellow lepers." He was now truly one of them.

Game Show Trivia

Watching the reactions of family members who may be hearing hurtful truths from their loved ones for the first time is part of the "appeal" of the show.

Game Show Trivia

Here are some sample questions that appeared on *The Moment of Truth*:

Have you ever lied to get a job?
Do you like your mother-in-law?
Do you really care about starving children in Africa?
Ever stolen anything from work?
Have you ever cheated on your spouse?

In addressing Saul as brother, Ananias was letting Saul know that they truly were connected; that Saul was now one of them—one of the Way.

In light of this amazing act of service by Ananias, it's really not surprising to read what happened next. "Immediately, something like scales fell from Saul's eyes, and he could see again" (Acts 9:18).

I hope you can see that God has a plan for your life.

I hope you can see that you are needed in this world.

I hope you can see the amazing things that can happen if you will answer when God calls, "Go!"

We're at the end of this book, and you're at a moment of truth. Are you happy where you are? Are you content to just sit in the studio audience?

I hope not, because you're needed on center stage.

Are you ready? Then come on down!

It's time to go!

Truth or Consequences

For individual or group study

For Personal Study and Reflection

List your top five favorite places to eat.

1.
2.
3.
4.
5.

Now circle the name of the restaurant that gives you the best service. Take a moment and list the three things that make the service you receive in that restaurant so special.

1.
2.
3.

Review your list and reflect on this question: Could those three things be used to describe the way you serve others?

For Group Study and Discussion

(Items needed: meal preparation) Conclude this study with a special meal for your small group. Give your group the best service possible. After dinner, ask your group to describe what they liked best about the service they received. Before continuing with the rest of this study, ask your group to reflect on this question: How would this world be different if we served others the way we were served tonight?

Truth

Read Acts 9:1-31.

1. Usually a moment of truth provides you with a clear choice to make.
Share or reflect on a time when you found yourself at a moment of truth. What were the choices you were facing at that time? How did the choice you made impact your life?

2. [Mark and I] both know—from personal experience—that we are serving a God of possibilities. We aren't serving a "no" God. With God there's always a way, so there is no way I'm going to tell him no.
Share or reflect on a time when God made a way where there appeared to be no way. What did you learn about life from that experience? What did you learn about God from that experience?

3. I hope you can see the amazing things that can happen if you will answer God's call, "Go!"
Share or reflect on one thing that you see more clearly now than you did before beginning this study. Decide on one thing you're going to change in your life based on this study.

Consequences

Share or reflect on one thing you learned in this chapter about:

- yourself

- God

How will you use the lessons from this chapter to bring about positive consequences in the lives of the people in your world? Be specific.

Acknowledgments

For me there's nothing better than being able to serve a God who gives everybody a chance to "Come on down!" . . . to join him on center stage, experience exciting adventures, and receive amazing treasures. One of the most exciting adventures in my life is the chance to write books. This is my fourth. I'm so grateful that God continues to give me a chance to minister to people like you through books like these.

Of the treasured "prizes" I've received, my family and friends are at the top of the list. This project wouldn't have happened without the love and support of these people:

Rhonda, my wife—I adore you. Thanks for your constant love and support. Loves.

Ashton, Levi, Sylas, Payton—I'm so proud to be your daddy. May you always prefer the excitement of center stage to the comfort of the studio audience.

My mom, Linda Chambers—You are so special to me. If my life were a book dedicated to God, you need to know that you've written a significant part of each chapter.

Twila Sias—Thank you for believing in me, editing me, and ministering to me.

My in-laws, John and Mary Smith—Your lives and ministry are an inspiration to me.

Blythe Daniel, my agent—You represent me so well; I'm profoundly grateful. But you represent Christ even better. I'm so honored to be serving with you.

Dale Reeves, Lynn Pratt, and the rest of the team at Standard Publishing—You are the best. Thanks for another opportunity to join with you in ministry.

Friends who have blessed my life and helped to make this book a reality—I love you all: Joe and Sue Sutherland, Doctors Ben and Sheri Lerner, Mark Atteberry, Steve Jackson, Jason Woolard (thanks for the office space!), Tamela Hancock-Murray, Terry Davis, Andrew Peterson, the staff and elders at Journey Christian Church—Jeff Crane, Amber Foley, Teri Beaver, Mark Young, Delmar Schroeder (nice pic!), Bill Moxon, Alan Miller, Gary Hamilton—I'm Enjoying the Journey!

And to you, the reader—You don't know how much you mean to me. Thanks for reading my books. I look forward to meeting you one day on center stage.

Acknowledgments

Notes

Information for the Game Show Trivia feature was taken from the following sources: David Schwartz, Steve Ryan, and Fred Wostbrock, eds., *The Encyclopedia of TV Game Shows* (3d ed.; New York City: Checkmark Books, 1999); http://www.imdb.com (accessed August 25, 2008); M. J. Stephey, "A Brief History of the Fist Bump," *Time Magazine*, http://www.time.com (accessed June 5, 2008); http://en.wikipedia.org (accessed August 25, 2008); http://gameshows.about.com (accessed August 25, 2008).

Introduction

1. As reported on the Web sites: http://www.wftv.com (accessed August 25, 2008) and http://www.thestranger.com (accessed August 28, 2008).

Chapter 1

1. http://www.telegraph.co.uk (accessed August 25, 2008).
2. http://www.americasbestcompanies.com (accessed August 25, 2008).
3. Ibid.
4. Ibid.
5. Ibid.
6. http://www.surfersam.com (accessed August 25, 2008).
7. Ibid.
8. Ibid.

Chapter 2

1. http://www.foxnews.com (accessed August 25, 2008).
2. http://en.wikipedia.org (accessed May 6, 2008).
3. http://www.chasingthefrog.com (accessed May 6, 2008).

Chapter 3

1. http://blogs.publicopiniononline.com (accessed August 25, 2008) and http://www.denverpost.com (accessed August 25, 2008).
2. http://www.healingwords.com (accessed August 25, 2008).
3. http://www.denverpost.com (accessed August 25, 2008).

Chapter 4

1. *Uncle John's Legendary Lost Bathroom Reader* (Ashland, OR: Bathroom Readers' Press, 1999), 47.
2. Read about it at http://www.washingtonpost.com (accessed August 25, 2008) and view it at http://www.youtube.com/watch?v= aN28HOFwfIw (accessed August 27, 2008).
3. http://wcbstv.com (accessed August 25, 2008) and http://www.nytimes.com (accessed August 30, 2008).

Chapter 5

1. Watch the Armstrongs' historic appearance at http://www.youtube.com/watch?v=zd7eWKCOk-A. An interesting side note: Neil Armstrong did not see this recording until forty years after it originally aired.
2. According to "A Review of FBI Security Programs: Commission for Review of FBI Security Programs, March 2002." http://www.fas.org/irp/agency/doj/fbi/websterreport.html (accessed August 25, 2008).
3. To view Keith's appearance go to http://www.youtube.com/watch?v=foHRDsFL260 (accessed August 29, 2008).
4. This information on one of my heroes was gleaned from the following Web site: http://www.kfc.com (accessed August 25, 2008).

Chapter 6

1. Jim Lovell and Jeffrey Kluger, *Apollo 13* (Boston: Houghton Mifflin Company, 2006), 239–240.
2. Calvin Miller, *The Table of Inwardness* (Downers Grove, IL: InterVarsity Press, 1984), 26.
3. I gleaned these stories from a Wikipedia article on *The Deadliest Catch*: http://en.wikipedia.org (accessed August 25, 2008).
4. http://www.alaskanfishingemployment.com (accessed August 25, 2008).
5. Stephen (Acts 7); Peter (according to church tradition Peter died in the persecution by Nero); Polycarp (He lived between AD 70 and 155. Polycarp was arrested on the charge of being a Christian. He was urged to proclaim Caesar as Lord if he wanted to save his life. Polycarp refused, even though he was told that his confession would free him from torture and execution. To this Polycarp responded, "Eighty-six years I have served Christ, and He never did me any wrong. How can I blaspheme my King who saved me?"

Polycarp refused to compromise his beliefs, and so was burned alive at the stake. For more information on Polycarp see: www.Polycarp.net, accessed August 30, 2008.)

6. http://en.wikipedia.org (accessed August 25, 2008).
7. Ibid.
8. http://www.christianitytoday.com (accessed August 25, 2008).
9. For more information: http://www.ciu.edu/news/chetbitterman (accessed August 25, 2008).
10. Rob Benson, "You Can Change the World!" at http://jmm.aaa.net.au/articles/18.htm (accessed August 29, 2008).
11. Ibid.
12. http://home.snu.edu (accessed August 25, 2008).

Chapter 7

1. http://www.ctv.ca (accessed August 25, 2008).
2. You can watch Marcil's embarrassing moment for yourself here: http://www.youtube.com/watch?v=xwR9e-PO2BM (accessed August 29, 2008).
3. http://www.usatoday.com (accessed August 25, 2008).
4. James S. Hewitt, ed., *Illustrations Unlimited* (Wheaton, IL: Tyndale House Publishers, Inc., 1988), p. 323.
5. According to a site devoted to Buddhist studies: http://www.buddhanet.net (accessed August 25, 2008).
6. I read about Muhammad's life and in particular his final years on this Web site: http://www.pbs.org (accessed August 25, 2008).

Chapter 8

1. http://yahoo.rogers.com (accessed August 25, 2008).
2. http://www.nypost.com (accessed August 25, 2008).
3. http://users.frii.com (accessed August 25, 2008).
4. As referenced in a devotion on *Christianity Today's* Web site: http://www.christianitytoday.com (accessed August 25, 2008).

Arron loves to hear from readers!
To contact him, or for more information about his speaking and writing ministry, visit the following:

www.arronchambers.com
www.christianstandard.com/MyLordandMyBlog

Other books by Arron Chambers:

Remember Who You Are

Running on Empty: Life Lessons to Refuel Your Faith

Scripture to Live By: True Stories and Spiritual Lessons Inspired by the Word of God